African American
master
student
Profiles

Osborne Robinson, Jr.
Catonsville Community College

Houghton Mifflin Company
Boston   New York

Director of Student Success Programs: Barbara A. Heinssen
Associate Editor: Melissa L. Plumb
Editorial Assistant: Kim Robles
Associate Project Editor: Rachel D'Angelo Wimberly
Associate Production/Design Coordinator: Jodi O'Rourke
Senior Designer: Henry Rachlin
Manufacturing Manager: Florence Cadran

Printed in the U.S.A.

Library of Congress Catalog Card Number: 96-76952

ISBN: 0-395-79688-1

23456789-SB-02 01 00 99 98

Contents

Preface

Students entering into the fast-paced world of higher education are often overwhelmed by the myriad of topics, perspectives, professors, courses, and choices. There are many decisions students are required to make during their first year of college. These decisions create a newfound independence which most students embrace. However, independence without purpose, preparation, and planning is often the seed that gives birth to unforeseen difficulties. Without a focused plan of action, students may struggle unsuccessfully with finances, relationships, schedules, classes, and teachers. In the midst of such struggles, the joy of the educational journey can be lost.

So, Why *African American Master Student Profiles*?

African American Master Student Profiles was developed to help restore to students the joy of the educational journey. It is suitable for use in any student success or freshman orientation course using *Becoming a Master Student* by David B. Ellis. It is also appropriate for student success courses where African American issues are addressed, and for non-student success courses, such as sociology (race and ethnic relations), English literature, African American Studies, or courses in diversity. Essentially, this book is appropriate wherever and whenever students need inspiration.

African American Master Student Profiles allows students a view of the extraordinary accomplishments of ordinary people, with a focus on transforming obstacles into opportunity. By providing glimpses into the lives of ordinary people who have accomplished extraordinary feats, the profiles will prompt students to:

- **work on and through issues of self-esteem, race, sexism, creativity, politics, and even tragedy** The principles, values, issues, and situations presented are useful for classroom discussion and life application.
- **participate in lively discussion, self-reflection, and group interaction, while becoming individually motivated** Learning by example from those who have already achieved greatness, as well as from their classmates, can offer students the motivation they need to succeed.
- **learn about and see in action varied writing styles and manners of self-expression** The varied styles of the profiles will engage students with some familiar styles of writing and expose them to other writing styles they may never have seen. In some profiles I have combined excerpts and narrative, while other profiles I have written entirely myself.
- **consider and answer *Questions,* either verbally or through written assignments**
- **read and explore outside of class, choosing from a list of *Selected Readings* presented for each profile** *Video Resources* are suggested, where applicable, to supply the opportunity for a multi-media view of those subjects profiled.

Everyday People . . . Extraordinary People

The twenty personalities profiled in *African American Master Student Profiles* come from a wide range of fields and disciplines, including academics, the arts, sports, politics, and business. In some cases, the profiled person was the first of their race to accomplish feats considered ground-breaking for African Americans or for society in general.

However, one thing that all the people profiled—whether they have already been successful or are on their way to becoming more successful—have in common with students is struggle. Their journeys have not been without adversity. Most did not begin their journey with a desire to achieve great things. Some were simply catapulted into the arena of achievement by circumstances or a desire to do something about some unfair or unjust experiences. Others responded to the call of competition. Still others responded to an inner witness that compelled them to be the best they could possibly be.

In each and every case, a strong survival instinct, a winning attitude to become more than just the renters

of someone else's vision, and a desire to be the crafters of their own destiny have led these ordinary people to become extraordinary examples of success. Each of the people profiled took action and responsibility for their lives. From Frederick Douglass, who was born a slave, to Magtanggol "Bong" Delrosario, who was born with a crippling disability, to Maya Angelou, who as a child did not speak for several years following a traumatic experience, somehow they all learned the art of taking action and transforming adversity into opportunity.

Student Action and Responsibility

Early in their academic careers, students also need to take responsibility and action for their destiny and their joy. The college experience is one of risk, discovery, achievement, growth, and hard work. The models highlighted in *African American Master Student Profiles* illustrate examples to follow and pitfalls to avoid. It is the responsibility of each student to dig deep into these profiles and discover for themselves the hidden truths that come through sacrifice and hard work. Clearly, the profiles shout that struggle, planning, achievement, hard work, and a positive attitude are a necessary part of the process of success.

Success Is a Choice

We want to engage today's students where they live. After working for twenty-five years in higher education, it is my professional opinion that *decisions (good or bad) determine destiny*. Mediocrity is not a choice. Successful students must learn to plan well and to navigate through uncertain and difficult times. They must learn to become students of excellence. They must learn to become planners of hope and to take action to secure their proper place in a future based on hope.

It is my desire to inform, stimulate, inspire, and challenge students by providing a range of diverse personalities in these profiles. It is my hope that the experiences of these personalities will teach students to take a course of action, move effectively through the obstacles and opportunities they face, and then experience victorious achievement. If students who have detoured from the road to success embrace the personalities in these profiles, they will enjoy an adventure that redirects, resuscitates, and rekindles their joy of education and their dreams. If students on the road to success embrace the personalities in these profiles, they will be challenged and encouraged to push, push, push toward their success, joy, and dreams.

Acknowledgments

I would like to thank my family and friends for all their encouragement and continuous support. I would like to extend my lasting gratitude to Alison Zetterquist for her insight in recognizing the need for such a project. I would like to thank my colleagues, Dave Ellis, the College Survival staff, and especially Barbara A. Heinssen, Melissa Plumb, Njia Lawrence-Porter, and Rachel D'Angelo Wimberly for their patience, time, and great suggestions.

I also thank the reviewers for their fine suggestions: Kathy Elaine Blanchard, Cuyahoga Community College (OH); Carolyn Buck, San Diego Mesa College (CA); Joyce Conoly-Simmons, City College of New York (NY); Nora Davis Day, Emory University (GA); Carlene H. Jackson, Delaware State University (DE); Ken Kirkpatrick, DePauw University (IN); C. Liegh McInnis, Jr., Jackson State University (MS); Clif McKnight, Quantum Success (MD); Jaqueline Richardson, Metropolitan State University (MN); Harry Rosemond, Green River Community College (WA); and Patricia L. Sheriff, Jackson State University (MS).

Maranatha!
Osborne Robinson, Jr.

Maya Angelou (1928–)
Activist, poet, speaker, and educator
Caged Birds Do Sing

The words of Maya Angelou—poet, lecturer, teacher, actress, songwriter, mother, and international diva—sometimes seem to whistle sonnets or give out jitterbug rhythms. They can tap-dance across the tracks of our tears, while weaving a powerful testament of our blood and pain: the African pain, the black pain, the white pain, the Navajo pain, the gay pain, the American pain, the pain that joins and binds. They remind us that caged birds do sing, and their songs are bittersweet songs.

Her words remind a great people of a great nation of their great failures. Yet the passion and poignancy of her words sing hope, hope that cannot be harnessed or hindered.

Look deep into the eyes of her pain, and you will see that Maya Angelou teaches high hope, which must be touched, tasted, and even taught. It is the kind of hope that is forged from oppression, chaos, and pain: hope that never stutters or stumbles, never surrenders the self to any internal or external tyranny.

Maya believes in the uncompromising power of the human spirit to overcome the travesties and tragedies of life. As you venture toward the vistas of Maya's own colorful life, look for the unexpected twists and turns, the tragedies and triumphs, that shape her extraordinary destiny. Then reflect on how unpredictable and fragile life really can be. Think about some of those unexpected circumstances that have already affected your destiny. Note how you responded to them: Were you angry, withdrawn, or hurt? Did you cry out for help? Just what *did* you do? These are the kinds of questions to consider as you journey into Maya Angelou's world.

Maya Angelou was born Marguerite Johnson on April 4, 1928, to Bailey and Vivian Johnson. They were divorced within three years of her birth. In her autobiography, *I Know Why the Caged Bird Sings,* Maya tells how she and her brother, who is a year older than she, were sent by train with a note that stated, "To Whom It May Concern . . . Marguerite and Bailey Johnson Jr., from Long Beach, California, [are] enroute to Stamps, Arkansas, c/o Mrs. Annie Henderson."

Arriving in the sleepy little southern town of Stamps, Arkansas, during the Great Depression of the 1930s, Maya and Bailey met their father's mother, a fiercely independent, strong, resourceful woman. Grandma Henderson was an unusual black woman who created a profitable business, selling pies to sawmill workers and to seed men at the local cotton gin. Her business savvy led her to build a general store in the Negro section of town, called the William Johnson General Merchandise Store.

Grandma Henderson owned that store for twenty-five years. It was the gathering place for the local townspeople and a place where Maya, Bailey, Grandma, and Maya's crippled Uncle Willie lived and made their living.

Maya just loved the comfort of the store when she, Bailey, Uncle Willie, and Grandma could just relax after a tiring day. This was the time when the four of them could just be family. (It also was the only time of the day when Uncle Willie did not shake or stutter.) Family always was important to Maya, and Grandma Henderson was the first, and probably the most important, mentor who taught her the essence of independence, courage, and hard work—knowledge that she would find steadying during rough times in her life.

When Maya was seven, she and Bailey went to live with their mother in St. Louis, Missouri. There, her mother's boyfriend, who had appeared to be a very kind and gentle man, began to molest young Maya and eventually rape her. This crushing betrayal by a man who the little girl had felt would protect and care for her affected her emotional health very seriously. With the additional trauma of the trial that followed and then the murder of the boyfriend, young Maya sank into depression that was as silent as it was deep. Because of guilt she felt regarding the accused man's death, she did not or could not speak, except rarely with her brother Bailey. And thus, this independent soul suffered alone. Accustomed to spreading her

wings and soaring above the down-to-earth aspects of life, Maya was now caged, her wings clipped, and—through no fault of her own—she felt cloaked in shame and pain. She had virtually closed down, closing out almost every adult in her family.

Initially, adult family members were very patient and sympathetic about Maya's condition; but after a doctor pronounced her physically healed, the family felt she should resume doing all the things that normal little girls were supposed to: running, jumping, and playing little-girl games. When Maya did not readily respond, she was considered stubborn, rebellious, and even insulting to the adults. Eventually, she was sent back to Grandma Henderson in Arkansas.

For several years in Arkansas, Maya was tormented from both within and without: from within, by the cringing, guilt-ridden mind of an innocent adolescent; from without, by the cruel, mean-spirited taunts of people who labeled her retarded. Yet Grandma Henderson's promise of a better day kept hope alive, for the older woman firmly believed that Maya would rise above the silence and despair.

During this period of silence, Maya met another powerful black woman of Stamps, Arkansas, someone with all the elegance, aristocratic manner, and poetry of an African queen. This small, gracious woman who spoke in a soft, melodious voice seemed the antithesis of Grandma Henderson, an imposing woman with a powerful voice and the largest hands for a woman that Maya had ever seen. Yet both women had the kind of strength that would influence Maya's life in profound ways.

Mrs. Bertha Flowers was the black nobility of Stamps, Arkansas. No one referred to Mrs. Flowers as Bertha, at least as far as Maya knew. Even in Maya's state of despair, she recognized the greatness in this woman who just by being herself, made her feel proud to be black. Mrs. Flowers, a teacher, was as genteel as any rich white woman of Stamps, Arkansas, and through reading aloud to Maya from great novels and poetry, she opened the young girl's world to the wonderful sounds of literature.

Maya fell in love with the works of great writers such as Shakespeare, Edgar Allan Poe, James Weldon Johnson, and Langston Hughes. She cherished the time that she and Bailey memorized Shakespeare's *The Merchant of Venice*. Although proud of their accomplishment, they were afraid to recite the play for Grandma because they would have to tell her that Shakespeare was white. In those days in the South, black folks had their heroes and white folks had *their* heroes and that was simply the way it was.

The power of the spoken word is very great. The silent girl responded with an insatiable appetite and started to memorize, recite, and dramatize fine literary works. Mrs. Flowers encouraged her to listen well to the rhythms of the parables that country folk would use to teach about "mother wit," the commonsense wisdom of generations. Eager to hear and practice the richness of spoken language, Maya had a reason to speak, and speak she did. Boldly, she emerged from her emotional devastation. She was stronger and wiser, with keen insight into what could conquer shame and guilt.

Maya Angelou became an outstanding honor student and made many friends. Life for her in Stamps, Arkansas, was finally precious and full of potential.

Maya and her brother eventually rejoined their mother in San Francisco, where, sadly, Maya's determination to be free led her for a time into such negative events as homelessness, teenage pregnancy, prostitution, drugs, unhappy marriage, and divorce. Yet despite these potentially crippling experiences, she never again closed down emotionally, never closed out help.

Finally, some doors began to open. A chance to become a dancer led to a career as a theatrical performer, which took Maya to Africa and Europe and seemed to be the start of a great career as an entertainer. But Maya did not stop there. She went on to write music, poetry, novels, and screenplays. Her gifts began to blossom after she learned not to hold them in but to give them to others.

Her varied experiences include working in the civil rights movement, marrying a South African freedom fighter, and living in Africa. Currently, Maya Angelou is an elder scholar who holds a lifetime appointment as a Reynolds Professor of American Studies at the prestigious Wake Forest University in Winston-Salem, North Carolina. Her many achievements, awards, acknowledgments, and successes speak of a life that shines. One of her best-known poems is a testament to hope: *And Still I Rise*.

SELECTED READINGS

Angelou, Maya. 1970. *I Know Why the Caged Bird Sings.* New York: Bantam Books.

Angelou, Maya. 1974. *Gather Together in My Name.* New York: Bantam Books.

Angelou, Maya. 1982. *The Heart of a Woman.* New York: Bantam Books.

Collections of Poems:

Angelou, Maya. 1975. *Oh Pray My Wings Are Gonna Fit Me Well.* New York: Random House.

Angelou, Maya. 1978. *And Still I Rise.* New York: Random House.

Angelou, Maya. 1988. *Shaker, Why Don't You Sing?* New York: Random House.

Angelou, Maya, 1990. *I Shall Not Be Moved.* New York: Random House.

Name _____   Date _____/_____/_____

QUESTIONS

1   *What does the phrase "caged birds sing" symbolize in Maya's life? Can you apply the phrase to some aspect of your life? Explain.*

2   *Have you had an experience where you felt unable to express yourself? What did you do about it? How do you think closing yourself down impedes your chances for success? Explain.*

3   *Isn't it sometimes the sound of silence in our valley of despair that imprisons us? What is your definition of self-imprisonment? Give some examples.*

4   *Have you had the opportunity to mentor someone who was isolating himself or herself from everyone else in the class? What did the instructor do to reach that person? What did you do?*

In some respects, I am a prisoner of the past. A long time ago, I made peace with the state of Virginia and the South. While I, like other blacks, was once barred from free association with whites, I returned time and time again, under the new rule of desegregation, to work with whites in my hometown and across the South. But segregation had achieved by that time what it was intended to achieve: It left me a marked man, forever aware of a shadow of contempt . . . across my identity and my sense of self-esteem. Subtly the shadow falls on my reputation, the way I know I am perceived; the mere memory of it darkens my most sunny days. I believe that the same is true for almost every African American of the slightest sensitivity and intelligence. Again, I don't want to overstate the case. I think of myself, and others think of me, as supremely self-confident. I know objectively that it is almost impossible for someone to be as successful as I have been as an athlete and to lack self-assurance. Still, I also know that the shadow is always there; only death will free me and blacks like me, from its pall.

The shadow fell across me recently on one of the brightest days, literally and metaphorically, of my life. On August 30, 1992, the day before the U.S. Open, the USTA (United States Tennis Association) and I together hosted an afternoon of tennis at the National Tennis Center in Flushing Meadows, New York. The event was a benefit for the Arthur Ashe Foundation for the Defeat of AIDS. Before the start, I was nervous. Would the invited stars (McEnroe, Graf, Navratilova, et al.) show up? Would they cooperate with us, or be difficult to manage? And, on the eve of a Grand Slam tournament, would fans pay to see light-hearted tennis? The answers were all a resounding yes (just over ten thousand fans turned out). With CBS televising the event live and Aetna having provided the air time, a profit was assured. The sun shone brightly, the humidity was mild, and the temperature hovered in the low 80s.

What could mar such a day? The shadow of race, and my sensitivity, or perhaps hypersensitivity, to its nuances. Sharing the main stadium box with Jeanne [Ashe's wife], Camera [his daughter], and me, at my invitation, were Stan Smith, his wife Marjory, and their daughter Austin. The two little girls were happy to see one another. During Wimbledon in June, they had renewed their friendship when we all stayed near each other in London. Now Austin, seven years old, had brought Camera a present. She had come with twin dolls, one for herself, one for Camera. A thoughtful gesture on Austin's part, and on her parents' part, no doubt. The Smiths are fine, religious people. Then I noticed that Camera was playing with her doll above the railing of the box, in full view of the attentive network television cameras. The doll was the problem; or rather, the fact that the doll was conspicuously a blond. Camera owns dolls of all colors, nationalities, and ethnic varieties. But she was now on national television playing with a blond doll. Suddenly I heard voices in my head, the voices of irate listeners to a call-in show on some "black format" radio station. I imagined insistent, clamorous callers attacking Camera, Jeanne, and me:

"*Can you believe the doll Arthur Ashe's daughter was holding up at the AIDS benefit? Wasn't that a shame?*"

"*Is that brother sick or what? Somebody ought to teach that poor child about her true black self!*"

"*What kind of role model is Arthur Ashe if he allows his daughter to be brainwashed in that way?*"

"*Doesn't the brother* understand *that he is corrupting his child's mind with notions about the superiority of the white woman? I tell you, I thought we were long past that!*"

The voices became louder in my head. Despite the low humidity, I began to squirm in my seat. What should I do? Should I say, To hell with what some people might think? I know that Camera likes her blond dolls, black dolls, brown dolls, Asian dolls, Indian dolls just about equally; I know that for a fact, because I have watched her closely. I have searched for signs of racial partiality in her, indications that she may be dissatisfied with herself, with her own color. I have seen none. But I cannot dismiss the voices. I try always to live practically, and I do not wish to hear such comments on the radio. On the other hand, I do not want Austin's gift to be sullied by an ungracious response. Finally, I act.

"Jeanne," I whisper, "we have to do something."

"About what?" she whispers back.

"That doll. We have to get Camera to put that doll down."

Jeanne takes one look at Camera and the doll and she understands immediately. Quietly, cleverly, she makes the dolls disappear. Neither Camera nor Austin is aware of anything unusual happening. Smoothly, Jeanne has moved them on to some other distraction.

I am unaware if Margie Smith has noticed us, but I believe I owe her an explanation. I get up and go around to her seat. Softly I tell her why the dolls have disappeared. Margie is startled, dumbfounded.

"Gosh, Arthur, I never thought about that. I never *ever* thought about anything like that!"

"*You* don't have to think about it," I explain. "But it happens to us, in similar situations, all the time."

"All the time?" She is pensive now.

"All the time. It's perfectly understandable. And it certainly is not your fault. You were doing what comes naturally. But for us, the dolls make for a bit of a problem. All for the wrong reasons. It shouldn't be this way, but it is."

I return to my seat, but not to the elation I had felt before I saw that blond doll in Camera's hand. I feel myself becoming more and more angry. I am angry at the force that made me act, the force of racism in all its complexity, as it spreads into the world and creates defensiveness and intolerance among the very people harmed by racism. I am also angry with myself. I am angry with myself because I have just acted out of pure practicality, not out of morality. The moral act would have been to let Camera have her fun, because she was innocent of any wrongdoing. Instead, I had tampered with her innocence, her basic human right to act impulsively, to accept a gift from a friend in the same beautiful spirit in which it was given.

Source: Arthur Ashe and Arnold Rampersad, *Days of Grace, a Memoir.* (New York: Ramada House, 1993)

SELECTED READINGS

Ashe, Arthur. 1988. *A Hard Road to Glory: A History of the African-American Athlete Since 1946.* New York: Amistad Press.

Ashe, Arthur, and Frank Deford. 1981. *Portrait in Motion.* New York: New American Library.

Ashe, Arthur, and Arnold Rampersad. 1993. *Days of Grace: A Memoir.* New York: Random House.

Sifford, Charlie. 1992. *Just Let Me Play: The Story of Charlie Sifford, the First Black PGA Golfer.* Latham, NY: British-American Publishing.

Name _____   Date _____/_____/_____

QUESTIONS

1 Do you believe that most Americans are hypersensitive about issues regarding race? On a personal level, have you feared being ostracized by your friends or peers because of your decision to befriend or date someone of another race? What did you do to reduce your fear?

2 Do you think Arthur Ashe's response to his daughter's playing with the blond doll was reasonable behavior? Why or why not?

3 Could this same hypersensitive attitude occur in relating to people with different sexual orientations? If your answer is yes, how—in your view—could someone deal with the oversensitivity?

4 What do you think Arthur Ashe learned from this incident? What did you learn from the incident or from a similar one that occurred in your life? Please share the circumstances, if you can, with other class members. How did you feel after the incident in your life occurred? What did you do? How did the other person or persons respond?

5 Think about developing a personal strategy that you will apply in your life to alleviate negative discrimination in your community.

Tyrone "Muggsy" Bogues (1965–)

Shortest player in National Basketball Association history

Live the Impossible Dream

Muggsy's conspicuous presence in the NBA has everything to do with overcoming the odds, everything to do with the little guy taking on and successfully competing with the big guy. His story is music to the ears of a young African-American entrepreneur, medicine against being discouraged by any prophets of doom. It is a story that speaks to the heart of each college student committed to the pursuit of personal excellence, a story that tells college graduates that if they are prepared they can compete against the best in corporate America. They can do well in the land of giants.

Patrick Ewing was shocked. I could see it in his eyes. The big, seven-foot center of the New York Knicks had come off a pick and received a pass near the top of the key. He positioned the ball in his right hand—his shooting hand. He pump-faked once to get Alonzo Mourning off his feet, squared his shoulders to the basket, eyed the target, brought the ball to his eyes, took a little jump, and prepared to fire.

He never saw me coming.

Whapppp!

In the small amount of time between Ewing catching the ball and shooting, less than a second, I came racing over from his right, timed my jump just right, got a good, clean takeoff, and swatted the ball away just before it left his shooting hand.

Patrick couldn't believe it. His shot had been blocked by someone whose head barely came up to the letters on his basketball jersey. Man, was he pissed!

I pounced on the loose ball and raced past him up court. I could see his expression—surprise, confusion, a little anger—but then I left him behind to start a fast break and score two points for us. On the way back down court, I ran up

to him, smiled my biggest smile, and said, "Thanks, big fella. Now you're on my highlight film."

All he could do was laugh. And keep an eye on me for the rest of the game.

The fans, of course, went crazy, but that's nothing new. Fans have always taken to me. It's been that way as long as I've been playing the game. I've always been a favorite of both home and away crowds. I'd like to think it's because I play so hard all the time I'm on the floor, that I play with intensity and passion, that I have fun on the court and I like to entertain the crowd. And I know in my heart that is all part of it.

Mostly, though, it is because I am five feet, three inches tall.

In my mind, my size is no big deal. I've been playing against bigger guys my whole life. I've always been the smallest guy around, as a baby, as a little kid, in high school. I think I stopped growing altogether by the time I was ten years old. To be honest, it seems like I've been five-three my whole life. I don't ever remember growing. In elementary school I was five-three. It's strange, isn't it? I think my mom was the first woman ever to give birth to a five-three baby.

But other people make a big deal of my size, especially in comparison to the guys I play against. See, to me, those other guys are just "footers": six-footers, seven-footers, and probably eight-footers someday. But I never believed only "footers" could play the game of basketball. People have always tried to tell me that, of course. From the first day I picked up a basketball, they told me to give it up. I was too small. I'd never make it. It was hopeless, no matter how good I was. I had to be big to play.

I never listened to any of them. To me, basketball is about talent, and heart, and desire. It's not about size. It's not a game for people who are big. It's a game for people who can play.

Tyrone Curtis Bogues—five feet, three inches of pure power, speed, and court savvy—is the shortest man in the NBA. And pound for pound, he is the best point guard in the history of the game and a sure shot for basketball's Hall of Fame.

Starting in scholastic sports as an excellent wrestler, Bogues has never been intimidated by the size of his opponents or by the toughness of their game. His mental and physical skills were sharpened on the competitive and often perilous playgrounds of

Baltimore. He attended Baltimore's Dunbar High School, where he played with present NBA stars David Wingate and Reggie Williams, and with Reggie Lewis, a Boston Celtics star who died young. And Bogues was learning more about basketball than just how to play it:

I learned early on that basketball was best used as a tool to help you get other things. In the ghetto, basketball—all sports really—is more than just a game. It's a way of life. For many kids, it's the only thing around to keep you out of trouble. But this way of life attracted some undesirable things to it, because successful people always draw a bad element that wants to be a part of that success. As a result, no matter how successful you might become, you always have to keep focused on making the next step. If you get caught up into the lifestyle of the moment, you are in danger. There are a ton of examples of people who lost sight of where they wanted to go, and suffered for it.

As Muggsy was growing up, Baltimore basketball was gaining national recognition. College scouts were coming from all over to see some of the best young talent in the nation. At their first sight of Muggsy, coaches often were amused by this pestering, pesky little ball hawk who could snatch a basketball and change the tide of a mundane, boring game. But the more they witnessed his play, the more they realized that this was an exceptional young athlete with a strong competitive spirit and a willingness to win.

He has always mystified his detractors and fascinated his admirers. His athletic feats are legendary, even inspirational. From Dunbar High School to Wake Forest University in Durham, North Carolina, where in his senior year (1986–1987) he led his team in scoring, to the elite play of the NBA, Bogues's reputation loomed large.

Like a David slaying a Goliath, each time he steps onto an NBA court, each time he makes a basket and gives an assist, he slays another myth about basketball's being just a big man's game, a game that can be played and dominated only by the likes of Wilt Chamberlain, Kareem Abdul Jabbar, or Michael Jordan. What he's said to each of us in the way he lives and in what he has accomplished is, Don't believe the hype, don't believe the doomsday prognosticators who tell you you're dreaming a truly impossible dream. Dream your

dreams, play your game, run your race, 'cause life ain't just about what you have and how you look. Life is about who you really are.

In one way or another, most of us live, play, and even struggle in some type of "land of giants." And not all Muggsy Bogue's giants have been related to size. At Wake Forest, he encountered a different type of challenge.

I have to say that I never experienced any racism, either on campus or in town. I want to be clear about that. Whenever I had problems with some of the professors or other students, whenever I felt they weren't giving me a fair deal, I never thought it was a racial thing so much as it was bias against athletes.

I felt more pressure on me there than I ever felt in my life. On the court I was safe. Off the court was the pressure. I was trying to maintain my studies, reading forty chapters in a week or two, working with tutors in every subject—not just one subject, every subject. I had practice two hours a day, study hall after classes, tutors after study hall—it was intense. My schoolwork was devastating. I had just never experienced the amount of work they required—so much reading, so many papers and exams. The professors covered more in a day than I had covered in a week in high school. I thought back on all my high school teachers who had tried to warn me. I wasn't prepared for this. Some of it was my own fault for coasting through high school. Some of it was simply that city schools aren't capable of competing with rich prep schools. But placing blame isn't the issue; the bottom line was, I struggled.

Some of his other giants had been the circumstances of living in a drug-infested housing project with a mother who was struggling to raise several children by herself. His father was in prison for attempted robbery. But to his parents' credit, they were good parents. His mother returned to school and earned a high school diploma, and his dad consistently wrote from the house of correction, encouraging his son to follow a straight and narrow path.

Our own giants may not be seven feet, two inches of living, walking, talking flesh. Our giants may not be sports announcers, players, or fans. Yet our giants may be poverty, disability, doubt, depression, pride, or despair. Instead of being a manager who believes we're

too short to play for his team, our giant may be a bruised and even brutalized spirit that whispers silent messages repeatedly each day, that we are inferior, unworthy, and unwanted. These giants wherever they exist, no matter how obvious or unapparent they may be, can block our vision and defeat our hope. They may be dominating us, controlling how we play in the game of life, and because of them we may develop low aim and small expectations. Bogues's life, though, teaches those of us who at times feel too small and too insignificant to make a difference, that we have to think big, play bigger, and aim higher than the way we feel.

Source: From *In the Land of Giants* by Tyrone "Muggsy" Bogues. Copyright © 1994 by Tyrone "Muggsy" Bogues and David Levine. By permission of Little, Brown and Company.

SELECTED READINGS

Bogues, Tyrone "Muggsy," and David Levine. 1994. *In the Land of Giants: My Life in Basketball, Vol. 1.* New York: Little, Brown & Company.

Graham, Lawrence Otis. 1995. *Member of the Club: Reflections on Life in a Racially Polarized World.* New York: HarperCollins Publishers, Incorporated.

Jackson, Phil, and Hugh Delehanty. 1995. *Sacred Hoops: Spiritual Lessons of a Hardwood Warrior.* New York: Hyperion Publishers.

Jordan, Michael. 1994. *I Can't Accept Not Trying: On the Pursuit of Excellence.* Harper San Francisco.

Name _____ Date _____/_____/_____

QUESTIONS

1 *Have you ever accomplished something that many people told you was impossible? Write a paragraph explaining what the situation was and how you felt when you succeeded. What do you think you learned from the experience?*

2 *Do you know of someone else in your family who overcame a major obstacle (perhaps a disability, or being a recent immigrant, or having a language problem, or facing discrimination)? How did that person's success affect the rest of the family—and you? Write a brief narrative explaining how your relative beat his or her personal giant(s).*

3 How does Muggsy Bogues's success inspire people to pursue their dreams, regardless of what others say? How do you deal with unwanted advice from able, professional people such as academic advisers, counselors, or family members, especially if they disagree with your choices?

4 What kind of success strategies could you develop from reading about Muggsy Bogues's life? List and explain several of them.

5 Do you think that for minorities and women, competing in corporate America is similar to Muggsy's playing in the NBA? If so, how?

Ronald Harmon Brown
(1941–1996)

First African-American Secretary of Commerce; first African-American chairman of the Democratic Party

Going the Distance

Ronald Harmon Brown, the first African-American Secretary of Commerce, was one of the consummate long-distance runners in the fields of law, business, and politics. He was an extremely focused, confident, skillful, and charismatic leader.

He moved among the rich and powerful with ease, never once forgetting his roots. Even as he died in a plane crash in remote Bosnia, he was going the distance for his country, carrying the torch of the American dream to a war-torn nation. And even in death, the elegance and splendor of this native son reached beyond nationalistic boundaries and touched the hearts of people everywhere.

Ron Brown was born in Washington, D. C., to William and Gloria Brown, both graduates of Howard University. The family moved to New York City when he was relatively young. His father managed the legendary Hotel Theresa in Harlem. Here, Ron encountered the social, artistic, political, and powerful elite of the African-American community. He encountered people who ran the race of life brilliantly, daring to be first in what they did. They were people like Jackie Robinson, the first African American to play professional baseball; W. E. B. Dubois, one of the first African Americans to receive a Ph.D. from Harvard; Duke Ellington, one of the first African Americans to own and lead an internationally acclaimed big band; Ralph Ellison, one of the first widely successful African-American writers; Adam Clayton Powell, the first African-American congressman from Harlem. Young Ronald Brown learned well the strategies of struggle, the power of struggle, and the peace in struggle. He was learning from these pioneers that sometimes the race is long and lonely, but it can be won by those who endure.

These were just a few of the multitalented and influential African-American long-distance runners who darted in and out of Ron's life on a frequent basis. It was at the Hotel Theresa that his unshakable confidence in himself and his people began to develop. This early life experience prepared him for the world at large. He learned from people like Jackie Robinson that in order to strive ahead, a person of vision must learn to stand alone. He learned that the door of success sometimes opens only one way, for one person at a time, and that person must be prepared to go first and go alone. Often as he peered out of the twelfth floor window of the Hotel Theresa, and observed the hustle and bustle of 125th St. below, he realized how easy it was to get lost in the superficial crowd of everyday life. He realized that the view from the top was a little better than the view from the bottom and that the Hotel Theresa with its legendary reputation and world famous clientele was simply his personal tutoring ground, training him to see above and beyond the crowded streets of New York City.

From the many heated discussions that Ron was involved in at the Hotel Theresa, Ron developed an agile mind and a disciplined tongue. He became almost invincible in his ability to present sound and convincing arguments. In this black cultural mecca, he studied how creative, artistic, and powerful African-American people behaved. He learned early that hard work, commitment, and perseverance characterized people of position and power. He learned the importance of appearance, preparation, and personal influence in the race called life, as he listened intensely to the guests' lively stories and daring escapades of world travel.

Life at the hotel created in him a positive view of people beyond the Hotel Theresa, beyond Harlem, even beyond America. Thus he was able to transcend any cultural shock when his parents sent him across town to the elite private schools of white New Yorkers. With this cross-cultural adaptability, Ron Brown possessed an invaluable skill that he would use time and again, as he moved confidently and skillfully through the corridors of power in black and white America. Fortunate in having encountered the best of both worlds, he became comfortable and successful in both.

Ron Brown didn't believe that it is necessary to abandon one's roots in order to succeed in the

dominant culture. Instead, he thought of knowledge as the key to success. He had an insatiable appetite for knowledge, along with a healthy perspective of who he was and what he could do, given the opportunity.

With this strong sense of self and the willingness to seek different academic and cultural experiences, he got himself accepted by Middlebury College in rural Vermont. This was significant, in that Middlebury was the first college known to have graduated an African American (Alexander L. Twight, in 1823). At Middlebury, far from the blacktop boulevards and the high-rise tenements of Harlem, Ron really began to excel. He was the first black initiated into the Middlebury chapter of the national, all-white fraternity Sigma Phi Epsilon, which eventually lost its national charter because of his induction.

Ron's gallant efforts to join Sigma Phi Epsilon had been a "significant first" that led to the elimination of racial barriers in campus-wide organizations. Many of his friends were doubtful that his initiation into Sigma Phi Epsilon would take place—but even here, Ron's influence seemed to set a standard.

Upon graduating in 1962 from Middlebury, Ron received an ROTC commission as a second lieutenant in the army, where he attained the rank of captain. After leaving the army, he became a social worker and attended law school at night at New York's St. Johns University. At St. Johns he met Mario Cuomo, former governor of New York, who was his law professor and mentor. Their association lasted some twenty years until Brown's untimely death. (The longevity and value of that friendship was apparent in 1992, when Governor Cuomo was asked by Brown to deliver the nominating speech at the Democratic National Convention for a then-unknown governor of Arkansas, William Jefferson Clinton. Brown had supported Clinton's candidacy when Brown became the first African-American chairman of the Democratic Party.)

Ron Brown's roster of firsts continued: he became the first African-American partner in the high-powered, high-profile Washington, D. C. law firm of Patton, Boggs, and Blow. He made his pilgrimage into national politics when he became Senator Edward M. Kennedy's deputy presidential campaign manager in 1968. Hard work and relentless self discipline helped make him the first black chairman of the Democratic National Committee. For his uncompromising and productive efforts, he was selected by President Clinton to a cabinet-level position as the first African-American Secretary of Commerce.

Paramount in Ronald Harmon Brown's strategies for success was knowing how to solicit trust from himself. He learned early to accept himself for who he was and what he could or couldn't do. Knowing his own strengths and weaknesses, he never shortchanged himself. He learned self-reliance by preparing for every area of his life. He was confident in his ability to lead, orchestrate, mediate, and guide. He knew the importance of building lasting relationships.

Going the distance, as far as Ron Brown was concerned, meant being properly prepared and then trusting himself to do his best. He had learned from the best and did not hinder himself with shortsighted thinking. He had learned to trust his ability, whether other people believed in him or not.

He was a man who learned not to get in his own way. So often we can become a greater hindrance to ourselves, more than racism, sexism, or any other kind of "ism." A healthy and confident attitude about our gifts, talents, and skills will certainly enable us to achieve our dreams.

Ron Brown's life shouts to each of us, "Be your own best cheerleader. Root for a winner. Be that winner yourself."

SELECTED READINGS

Covey, Steven R. 1989. *The Seven Habits of Highly Effective People.* New York: Simon & Schuster.

Frisby, Michael. 1996. "Standard Bearer." *Emerge* (June pp. 30–37).

Johnson, James Weldon, and Kathryn S. Wilson. 1995. *The Selected Writings of James Weldon Johnson: New York Age Editorials (1914–1923).* New York: Oxford University Press, Incorporated.

Wickham, Dewayne. 1995. *Woodholme: A Black Man's Story of Growing Up Alone.* New York: Farrar, Straus, & Giroux, Incorporated.

Questions

1 *Give an explanation for the title of this selection.*

2 *How do you believe Ron utilized mentors in his life? Do you have mentors in your life? How do you use those mentors?*

3 *Why was Ron's cross-cultural experience vital to his success?*

4 *Have you had any cross-cultural or multicultural experiences? Write an essay on their benefits and the pitfalls.*

5 *What theme do you believe this profile of Ron Brown conveys about his attitude and experiences?*

Benjamin Carson (M.D.) (1951–)

Chief pediatric neurosurgeon, Johns Hopkins

Higher Calling

More blood! Stat!"

The silence of the [operating room] was smashed by the amazingly quiet command. The twins had received 50 units of blood, but their bleeding still hadn't stopped!

. . . A quiet panic erupted through the room. Every ounce of type AB negative blood had been drained from the Johns Hopkins Hospital blood bank. Yet the 7-month-old twin patients who had been joined at the back of their heads since birth needed more blood or they would die without ever having a chance to recuperate. This was their only opportunity, their only chance, at normal lives. . . .

Many of the 70-member team began offering to donate their own blood, realizing the urgency of the situation. . . .

Fortunately, within a short time the city blood bank was able to locate the exact number of units of blood needed to continue the surgery. Using every skill, trick, and device known in their specialties, the surgeons were able to stop the bleeding within a couple of hours. The operation continued. Finally, the plastic surgeons sewed the last skin flaps to close the wounds, and the 22-hour surgical ordeal was over. The Siamese twins—Patrick and Benjamin—were separate for the first time in their lives!

The exhausted primary neurosurgeon who had devised the plan for the operation was a ghetto kid from the streets of Detroit. . . .

Ben Carson. Just an ordinary name—but one that is recognized and respected throughout America's medical community.

He is an not an ordinary person. His story may assist you in deciding how you would like to spend the rest of *your* life. As you learn about Ben's calling and listen to his words, think about whether you are still on track in fulfilling your own early dreams. If you're not on track, if you have some regret about your present direction, seriously explore the reasons for the decisions, events, or circumstances that have changed your life's path. Be sure to listen closely to Ben's following conversation with his mother because that conversation determined his destiny. He was twelve years old at the time and fascinated by the stories about missionary doctors he had been hearing at church.

"That's what I want to do," I said to my mother as we walked home. "I want to be a doctor. Can I be a doctor, Mother?"

"Bennie," she said, "listen to me." We stopped walking and Mother stared into my eyes. Then laying her hands on my thin shoulders, she said, "If you ask the Lord for something and believe He will do it, then it'll happen."

"I believe I can be a doctor."

"Then, Bennie, you will be a doctor," she said matter-of-factly, and we started to walk on again.

Benjamin Carson never forgot for one moment his dream of becoming a healer, a doctor, and he never stopped believing in himself and his plan. He was convinced that if he did well in school, the Lord would bless him and he would become a doctor. From his earliest teens, every thought, nerve, and muscle was focused on finishing high school and going to college.

College was to be the giant step. College would be the ticket to his life's work, and college was his target. Not just any college, either, but an Ivy League one where, Ben Carson knew, he would be a star and move closer to his calling. The day finally came: high school study, and certain sacrifices were all behind him and Ben was ready—or at least he thought he was ready—for Yale.

I strode onto the campus, looked up at the tall, gothic-style buildings, and approved of the ivy-covered walls. I figured I'd take the place by storm. And why not? I was incredibly bright. . . .

But I quickly learned that the classwork at Yale was difficult, unlike anything I'd ever encountered at Southwestern High School. The professors expected us to have done our homework before we came to class, then used that information as the basis for the day's lectures. This was a foreign concept to me. I'd slid through semester after

semester in high school, studying only what I wanted, and then, being a good crammer, spent the last few days before exams memorizing like mad. It had worked at Southwestern. It was a shock to realize it wouldn't work at Yale.

Each day I slipped farther and farther behind in my classwork, especially in chemistry. Why I didn't work to keep up, I'm not sure. I could give myself a dozen excuses, but they didn't matter. What mattered was that I didn't know what was going on in chemistry class.

It all came to a head at the end of the first semester when I faced final examinations. The day before the exam I wandered around the campus, sick with dread. I couldn't deny it any longer. I was failing freshman chemistry; and failing it badly. . . . As the realization sunk in of my impending failure, this bright boy from Detroit also stared squarely into another horrible truth—if I failed chemistry I couldn't stay in the premed program.

Despair washed over me as memories of fifth grade flashed through my mind. "What score did you get, Carson?" "Hey, dummy, did you get any right today?" Years had passed, but I could still hear the taunting voices in my head.

What am I doing at Yale anyway? It was a legitimate question, and I couldn't push the thought away. *Who do I think I am? Just a dumb Black kid from the poor side of Detroit who has no business trying to make it through Yale with all these intelligent, affluent students.* I kicked a stone and sent it flying into the grass. *Stop it,* I told myself. *You'll only make it worse.* I turned my memories back to those teachers who told me, "Benjamin, you're bright. You can go places." . . .

One glimmer of hope—a tiny one at that—shone through my seemingly impossible situation. Although I had been holding on to the bottom rung of the class from the first week at Yale, the professor had a rule that might save me. If failing students did well on the final exam, the teacher would throw out most of the semester's work and let the good final-test score count heavily toward the final grade. That presented the only possibility for me to pass chemistry.

Midnight. The words on the pages blurred, and my mind refused to take in any more information. I flopped into my bed and whispered in the darkness, "God, I'm sorry. Please forgive me for failing You and for failing myself." Then I slept.

. . .

The professor came in, and without saying much, began to hand out the booklets of examination questions. . . . At last, heart pounding, I opened the booklet and read the first problem. . . .

I knew the answer to every question on the first page. . . .

I was so excited to know correct answers that I worked quickly, almost afraid I'd lose what I remembered. Near the end of the test, . . . I didn't get every single problem. But it was enough. I knew I would pass.

. . .

During my four years at Yale I did backslide a little, but never to the point of not being prepared. I started learning how to study, no longer concentrating on surface material and just what the professors were likely to ask on finals. I aimed to grasp everything in detail. In chemistry, for instance, I didn't want to know just answers but to understand the reasoning behind the formulas. From there, I applied the same principle to all my classes.

After this experience, I had no doubt that I would be a physician. I also had the sense that God not only wanted me to be a physician, but that He had special things for me to do. I'm not sure people always understand when I say that, but I had an inner certainty that I was on the right path in my life—the path God had chosen for me. Great things were going to happen in my life, and I had to do my part by preparing myself and being ready.

Source: Taken from *Gifted Hands* by Ben Carson and Cecil Murphy. Copyright © 1990 by Review and Herald® Publishing Association. Used by permission of Zondervan Publishing House.

SELECTED READINGS

Carson, Benjamin, and Cecil B. Murphey, 1991. *Think Big: Discovering Your Gift of Excellence.* Grand Rapids, Mich.: Zondervan Publishing House.

Carter, Carol. 1990. *Majoring in the Rest of Your Life.* New York: Noonday Press.

Love, Spencie, and John Hope Franklin, 1997. *One Blood: The Death and Resurrection of Charles R. Drew.* Chapel Hill: University of North Carolina Press.

well some of the arias that Marian Anderson sang. But to have, for example, almost daily contact with writer and critic Arna Bontemps who was the university's librarian, was awe-inspiring. My days at Fisk also gave me an opportunity to experience a vibrant collage of African-American culture, from theatrical performances to art exhibits at the Fisk gallery to concerts by the Jubilee Singers.

. . .

In January 1953 my father died, and I was devastated by the loss. Hurt, confused, lonely, I decided to leave Fisk and transfer to Oberlin College. In retrospect, I was not running away from Fisk as much as from my father's death and toward my sister Marvyne who was then at Oberlin.

Oberlin was a culture shock, but in the end, an extraordinary intellectual experience for me. I was part of a little band of Black folk in a White sea. But it was a White sea that claimed to be a friendly one, and as one of the first American colleges to accept African-American and women students, Oberlin quite justifiably maintained that it had been a friendly sea for many, many years.

Oberlin was a startling, intriguing adventure that showed me just how narrow and closed the South had been, where Black is Black and White is White. Oberlin was the antithesis of that. For the first time I had to distinguish among white people: they weren't all Southern and Christian! It was also my first real opportunity to interact with people from China, Hawaii, and various African countries. . . .

When I entered Oberlin in the fall of 1953, I was still saying what I said since childhood in response to "What do you want to be when you grow up?" "A pediatrician." In those days if you were female, being a doctor usually meant being a pediatrician. Surely you could not be a surgeon—only boys grew up to become that. But one class, "Introduction to Cultural Anthropology," permanently put to rest for me the idea of a career in medicine.

On the first day of class, Professor George Eaton Simpson stood before us and began to simulate hyperventilation, moving his body to Jamaican revivalist cult music. Between breaths he talked about this music, Jamaican religious cults, and much of the culture that is in the Caribbean and throughout the Americas as expressions of African culture in the New World. This, he said, is what anthropologists study. For me, it was an immediate, passionate reaction: Good-bye pediatrics!

. . .

Oberlin did not offer an anthropology major, but I took every course offered in the field, majored in sociology, and became Simpson's special student. With time and study my interest in anthropology only deepened, and the idea of becoming an anthropologist proved more than a passing fancy with a newfound, hundred-dollar word. As a result, there was no question but that I would go on to graduate school in anthropology, for the sake of a career and, ultimately, for my own well-being. I had some serious questions about being Black in America, and anthropology was at least speaking to, if not answering these questions. As I have often said to my students, you can either go through life haphazardly trying to respond to questions that trouble you, or in an organized way you can seek answers. I chose the latter. . . .

At the same time that I chose the field of cultural anthropology, I also knew my particular interest was Africa. This, combined with the fact that George Simpson had a close relationship with anthropologist Melville J. Herskovits, meant there was only one place for me to go. I would study with Herskovits, the great scholar of African and African-American culture at Northwestern where I would eventually earn my M.A. and Ph.D. in anthropology.

Herskovits had two special places in his heart: one for students who were African American, and another for students who were women. Both were in very short supply in those days, but there I was—both an African American and a woman. More importantly, however, I was a serious student, ready to be mentored.

Johnnetta Cole blossomed under the tutelage of Melville Herskovits at Northwestern, but she needed and wanted more than textbook knowledge about African culture. She decided to venture to Liberia for a firsthand look at the African experience and to complete her field studies for her doctorate in anthropology. It was during those years in Liberia that for the first time in her life, she was able to experience the emotional, spiritual, and physical security of being a member of the majority race. However, it was also the first time she witnessed black-on-black political, social, and economic exploitation. To her, this was a profound revelation.

Upon leaving Liberia with her new consciousness, she returned to the United States and eventually took a teaching position in black studies at Washington State University. It was at Washington State University that she became involved with the civil rights and antiwar movements of the 1960s. But not until 1979 when she

went to work at the University of Massachusetts at Amherst as a professor of black studies and anthropology that the plague of sexism and gender issues began to capture her interest. Here, a lamp of consciousness was lit to show other young women the way to fight discrimination of any kind. As an anthropologist, her desire to study the effects of racism and sexism took her from the rich farm lands of Mississippi and Iowa to the soft blue waters of Haiti, St. Croix, and Cuba. She went from Cuba where she discovered less racism and more sexism to the halls of Hunter College where racism and sexism were more subtle yet still alive. It was at Hunter College in New York City where she was recruited for the presidency of Spelman College, an all women's college in Atlanta.

When my appointment was made it was clearly an historic moment for Spelman College and as I moved across the country speaking as Spelman's "Sister President," I came to see that this appointment belonged to all Black women. This school which originated in 1881 as the Atlanta Female Seminary in the basement of Friendship Baptist Church for the express purpose of educating African-American women had been led by four White women and two African-American men. There had never been an African-American woman president of this African-American women's college. For years Spelman students, faculty, and alumnae had been calling for a president who reflected the student body. Indeed, one doesn't have to work all that hard to see the deferment of this dream as a metaphor for the history of African-American women, and their struggle against racism and sexism.

. . .

Years later as I continue to mentor young African-American women anthropologists, I recall that when I was in college and graduate school I did not see myself reflected in the scholars who taught and encouraged me. I had to lean on the works of Zora Neale Hurston and St. Clair Drake to gain what all students surely profit from: evidence that if someone who looks like me has done it, surely so can I! . . . "Never mumble who you are."

Source: From *Conversations* by Johnnetta B. Cole. Copyright © 1993 by Johnnetta B. Cole. Used by permission of Doubleday, a division of Bantam, Doubleday Dell Publishing Group, Inc.

SELECTED READINGS

Broussard, Cheryl D. 1991. *The Black Woman's Guide to Financial Independence: Money Management Strategies for the 1990s.* Oakland, Calif.: Hyde Park Publishers.

Cole, Johnnetta B. 1994. *Conversations: Straight Talk with America's Sister President.* New York: Doubleday/Anchor Books.

Hitt, William D. 1992. *Thoughts on Leadership: A Treasury of Quotations.* Columbus, Ohio: Battelle Press.

Williams, Terrie, with Joe Cooney. 1994. *The Personal Touch: What You Really Need to Succeed in Today's Fast-Paced Business World.* New York: Warner Books, Incorporated.

Name _____ Date _____/_____/_____

Questions

1 *Why do you think getting involved with student-related activities will increase your possibility for success? List several ways you can get involved in extracurricular activities.*

2 *Give an example of someone who personifies the statement "Never mumble who you are." Explain your choice.*

3 *Johnnetta Cole realized that she preferred to study anthropology rather than medicine after she took an introductory class in anthropology. Have you decided what field to major in? Write about the different course majors you are considering: list and describe your reasons for considering each. Compare and contrast the benefits and the difficulties of each major. See if you can conduct an interview with someone working professionally in at least one of your career choices.*

4 *Johnnetta Cole says, "I recall that when I was in college and graduate school I did not see myself reflected in the scholars who taught and encouraged me." Do you think that environment has changed? Do you see anyone like you in the role that you want someday to be in?*

5 *List several ways to get to know the college officials who can assist you in accomplishing your educational goals. Look up the definition of* Mentor. *What qualities would you seek in a mentor?*

Magtanggol "Bong" Delrosario (1977–)

Student and award-winning videographer

Renaissance Man

As editor and compiler of this series of profiles, I enjoy sharing with readers the characteristics that qualify these individuals as master achievers. Here is one profile of an African-American student who is presently on the road to success. Like so many other young students who are full of potential, this young man is a diamond in the rough, and he is not a student who easily buys into the professorial wisdom of today. But he is one who, when challenged, rises to the occasion and produces works of excellence. Sometimes he surprises himself.

As I have worked with students over the last twenty years, I have discovered that at times, students can be tough to work with. Sometimes students are not what they seem to be. Sometimes they don't fit the mold of how a student "should" dress or speak. Yet when we encounter them the fire of potential may be hidden under layers of rejection, suspicion, and anger; it is a teacher's or a mentor's duty, if not our calling, to reach through the superficial, negative attitudes and release each student's gifts.

There are no perfect teachers or perfect students, only perfect moments or opportunities. As teachers and students, we need to seize the moment where giving and learning can best occur. If you are a student or a teacher, take a good look and see if you know a Mr. Delrosario. See if someone very like him is somewhere in your community or your school. See if there's a little or even a lot of Bong Delrosario in you.

When I first met Bong, it was a bright autumn day. I'll never forget it. As a matter of fact, it was September 8, 1995. I was teaching a student-success course for African-American males, and was just approaching the podium when suddenly a speeding flash in a wheelchair darted through the classroom door, shouting, "Yo, sorry, professor; I'm sorry I'm late for your class and I know it's the first day." This happened so quickly that I almost didn't know if the chair was talking or was occupied by some speeding alien, or if we were being invaded by some rap artist on wheels. But here was a big brown clear-eyed character with wavy black hair and a mischievous grin, storm-rolling into my classroom, late!

I wanted to respond in a very cool professorial manner, with "Young man, just be seated," but of course he already *was* seated, ensconced like some proud king in a motorized chariot. And he had maneuvered his vehicle down the aisle, past several rows of students, and come to a screeching halt in front of an empty desk. For a brief moment there was complete silence in the room; then he said, "Yo, professor; yo professor; what's your name?"

What's my name, yo, what's my name; who is this character? I said to myself, aware that a puzzled look must have appeared on my face.

"Oh, I'm sorry. Professor Robinson. I see it written on the blackboard. Excuse me, sir; I apologize, I apologize."

He apologizes; yeah, right!

Apology accepted, I immediately flipped the class roster to get a sense of whom I might be talking to.

"What's *your* name?" I grumbled.

"It's Bong, sir. Bong."

"What's your real name, young man? What's your name?" I deepened the pitch of my voice.

"Like I said, Professor Robinson, it's Bong; it's Bong Delrosario. It should be on the class roster, 'cause I registered for this class early."

And as he said that, "I glanced sharply in his direction and thought, This must be the one. Every semester, there's one. But this one is different; wheelchair and all, this one is really different.

That 's how we met. Bong Delrosario was born with congenital arthrogryposis; a disease that immobilizes the joints of the body, preventing full movement of the arms, wrists, and legs. Bong cannot kneel, cannot stretch or spread his legs, nor can he even move his fingers to write or to feed himself. When he was born, doctors said he would not live longer than three months; but he continues to defy conventional medical wisdom.

At eighteen, he had accomplished more than most teenagers or even adults. He doesn't deny that it is difficult to transfer from wheelchair to toilet, or from

bed to wheelchair, or that it is hard to get into his clothes (by rolling into them on the floor), or that it is complicated to write by holding a pen or pencil in his mouth. But Bong does deny, as he stated in discussions with me, the overwhelming power of the word *can't*, declaring instead,

I *can*, I can do things, but I just have to do them differently. When I run up against an obstacle, I just believe that there is always a way to deal with any obstacle. I might have to approach it differently but there is a way to win in any situation. I guess I got that attitude from my mother. You see, she is one of the most determined people I know. When I was born, my entire family including my father turned their backs on my mother because I was born disabled and they wanted my mother to rid herself of this helpless and hapless child. She didn't accept their opinions and she didn't care what people said about me or her. Today I'm the same way when people stare at me like I'm a statue or something. Or when they tell me I can't do this or become that. I look at them like they have braces on their brains.

When I was four years old, I became very conscious of how physically different I was from my friend Donnell, whom I have known since kindergarten. I really realized for the first time that I couldn't run and jump in the same way as Donnell. But my mother was determined to raise me, and to raise me to be independent and successful at whatever I chose to do in life. She was always honest with me about my disability; she would always tell me the facts and she refused to let me use my disability as an excuse not to try something. Nor would she permit me to pretend that I wasn't differently abled than other children. She taught me from the beginning to accept myself for myself, warts and all, the good and the bad, and to love myself. One thing for sure, whatever she tried to teach me to do, I always knew whether I succeeded or failed, she would still love me, not for what I could or couldn't do. I learned to love myself in the same way. My mother modeled and mentored love for me. I have the kind of strength and determination that permits me to approach life honestly and lovingly. I love people; I love to show people what anyone can do if they simply try.

When Donnell and I were approached by William Whiteford and Susan Cohen, documentary filmmakers who wanted to follow our relationship over a nine-year period, it was just unbelievable, that people wanted to make a film about our lives. [This documentary aired again on HBO in September 1997.] At that time, I thought this was the most exciting thing that ever happened to me. I was wrong. Years later when we were in high school, we were interested in making a video, but neither one of us realized that the video would have to be written , directed, starred in, and edited by us. We were just two high school students who had never done anything like this before. I began to think and struggle with whether or not I could really do this; but suddenly everything Mother had said, everything Mother had taught me, seemed to echo and vibrate in the deepest crevice of my being like a gentle voice across the Grand Canyon. It just began to swell up and repeat itself in me, like a force fueled by its own destiny. It began to take over; the determination, the love, the love of the challenge began to excite me and overwhelm me. I knew we could do it. I knew it despite the doubts, the dissing, the taunts and the jeers of everybody else; I just knew we would pull this off and we did! We wrote, directed, edited, starred in, and submitted it for national competition and we won. We won Golden Apple award, which is equivalent to the Oscar for Hollywood movie stars. Can you believe it; we won the high school "Oscar" for our video called *The Mall,* written and directed by Bong and Donnell, two young dudes from Baltimore. Man, I felt great, I felt strong, I felt like I just loved people. This was really the clincher for me. I mean, I had always known what Mother had taught me was true, but now I really knew for myself.

After we won the award for *The Mall,* there were several offers to appear on TV shows throughout the entire country. Donnell and I really enjoyed our first plane ride, all the travel and meeting all those nice people. We enjoyed our moment of stardom and our newfound celebrity status at school. It was like we were movie stars or something. It seemed that everybody wanted to know who we were, where we lived, and what we were doing. All we seemed to hear was "Bong and Donnell, Bong and Donnell."

We formed our own production company and I decided what I really wanted to do with the rest of my life. I wanted to be a clinical psychologist and a filmmaker, a person who would be a role model and motivator for people with physical disabilities. I wanted as I do now to show people that anybody can have a dream and that dream can come true. Doesn't matter if you are in a wheelchair; doesn't matter if you have to write with your pen in your mouth. But what does matter is that you have to believe in yourself whether you have a disability or not, that you have to love living with your disability by making it your friend and not your enemy!

Presently I am enrolled at a community college and after graduation, I will be going to the University of Maryland at Baltimore County (UMBC) to pursue a dual major in

psychology and filmmaking. I know it's not going to be easy, but so what; it *ain't* never been easy for me anyway. Whatever it takes to accomplish my goals, I know that I have what it takes to meet the challenge.

There is no question that Bong has seen great struggles and had many obstacles to overcome; but when he smiles, there isn't a hint of resentment about his disability or his life. When he smiles, his smile confidently and powerfully radiates who he is and what he can do. There is no shadow in that smile, only the sunshine of a gifted soul who has responded to the challenges of life with the spirit of victory. When the host of one TV show asked Bong if there was anything he could not do, Bong simply said, "Oh, yeah, I can't walk."

SELECTED READINGS

Beatty, Richard H. 1992. *One Hundred and Seventy-Five High-Impact Cover Letters.* New York: John Wiley & Sons.

Copage, Eric V. 1993. *Black Pearls: Daily Meditations, Affirmations and Inspirations for African Americans.* New York: William Morrow & Company, Incorporated.

Massie, Brigid McGrath, and John Waters. 1991. *What Do They Say When You Leave the Room? How to Increase Your Personal Effectiveness for Success at Work, at Home, and in Your Life.* Salinas, Calif.: Eudemonia Publications.

A Resource Manual for Developmentally Disabled Individuals and Their Advocates. 1980. Washington, D.C.: Office of Human Resources, Administration on Developmental Disabilities.

Name _____   Date _____/_____/_____

QUESTIONS

1 *Have any physically challenged people served as positive role models in your life?*

2 *How was Bong's mother a mentor and a positive role model for him? Has someone in your family been a mentor and a positive role model to you? Are you a mentor or a positive role model for someone in your family? Explain.*

3   Does Bong have a realistic view of his goals? Have you ever wondered what it would be like to spend just a day in a wheelchair? Have you considered how you would catch a bus or a train or just get around and meet people while in a wheelchair? Imagine yourself doing these things; then write a composition about your feelings and impressions during the "experience."

4   For what community does Bong want to be a positive role model? For what community would you like to be one? Why?

5   Do you have disabilities that you will not permit to get in the way of your success? Explain. Compile a list of the top ten success strategies that you use for your life. If you don't have any, begin today by creating some for your journey of success. Some of the strategies could pertain to goal setting, action planning, overcoming obstacles, and career planning.

Frederick Douglass (c. 1818–1895)

Abolitionist, writer, and orator; former slave

Freedom Begins with . . .

Frederick Augustus Washington Douglass was born into slavery, in Tuckahoe, Maryland, about 1818. On September 3, 1838, Frederick Douglass escaped to freedom. The powerful story of his exodus from slavery to freedom did not begin on that day, though. It had begun years earlier, when he witnessed a vicious verbal attack on his new mistress by her husband for teaching a slave child to read. In his autobiography, *Narrative of the Life of Frederick Douglass,* he tells how this incident changed not only his life but also the life of a woman who had been kind to him.

My new mistress proved to be all she appeared when I first met her at the door,—a woman of the kindest heart and finest feelings. She had never had a slave under her control previously to myself, and prior to her marriage she had been dependent upon her own industry for a living. She was by trade a weaver; and by constant application to her business, she had been in a good degree preserved from the blighting and dehumanizing effects of slavery. I was utterly astonished at her goodness. I scarcely knew how to behave towards her. She was entirely unlike any other white woman I had ever seen. I could not approach her as I was accustomed to approach other white ladies. My early instruction was all out of place. The crouching servility, usually so acceptable a quality in a slave, did not answer when manifested toward her. Her favor was not gained by it; she seemed to be disturbed by it. She did not deem it impudent or unmannerly for a slave to look her in the face. The meanest slave was put fully at ease in her presence, and none left without feeling better for having seen her. Her face was made of heavenly smiles, and her voice of tranquil music.

But, alas! this kind heart had but a short time to remain such. The fatal poison of irresponsible power was already in her hands, and soon commenced its infernal work. That cheerful eye, under the influence of slavery, soon became red with rage; that voice, made all of sweet accord, changed to one of harsh and horrid discord; and that angelic face gave place to that of a demon.

Very soon after I went to live with Mr. and Mrs. Auld, she very kindly commenced to teach me the A, B, C. After I had learned this, she assisted me in learning to spell words of three or four letters. Just at this point of my progress, Mr. Auld found out what was going on, and at once forbade Mrs. Auld to instruct me further, telling her, among other things, that it was unlawful, as well as unsafe, to teach a slave to read. To use his own words, further, he said, "If you give a nigger an inch, he will take an ell [forty-five inches]. A nigger should know nothing but to obey his master—to do as he is told to do. Learning would *spoil* the best nigger in the world. Now," said he, "if you teach that nigger (speaking of myself) how to read, there would be no keeping him. It would forever unfit him to be a slave. He would at once become unmanageable, and of no value to his master. As to himself, it could do him no good, but a great deal of harm. It would make him discontented and unhappy." These words sank deep into my heart, stirred up sentiments within that lay slumbering, and called into existence an entirely new train of thought. It was a new and special revelation, explaining dark and mysterious things, with which my youthful understanding had struggled, but struggled in vain. I now understood what had been to me a most perplexing difficulty— . . . the white man's power to enslave the black man. It was a grand achievement, and I prized it highly. From that moment, I understood the pathway from slavery to freedom. It was just what I wanted, and I got it at a time when I least expected it. Whilst I was saddened by the thought of losing the aid of my kind mistress, I was gladdened by the invaluable instruction which, by the merest accident, I had gained from my master. Though conscious of the difficulty of learning without a teacher, I set out with high hope, and a fixed purpose, at whatever cost of trouble, to learn how to read. The very decided manner with which he spoke, and strove to impress his wife with the evil consequences of giving me instruction, served to convince me that he was deeply sensible of the truths he was uttering. It gave me the best assurance that I might rely with the utmost confidence on the results which, he said, would flow from teaching me to read. What he most dreaded, that I most desired. What he most loved, that I most hated. That which to him was a great evil, to be carefully shunned, was to me a great good, to be

diligently sought; and the argument which he so warmly urged, against my learning to read, only served to inspire me with a desire and determination to learn. In learning to read, I owe almost as much to the bitter opposition of my master, as to the kindly aid of my mistress. I acknowledge the benefit of both.

This incident became a pivotal point in Frederick Douglass's life. Although he was still a child and remained with the Aulds for several more years, he became determined, with a singleness of purpose. He knew that regardless of the time it would take or the opposition he would face, he *would* learn to read. Reading had become very important in his life.

. . . I lived in Master Hugh's family about seven years. During this time, I succeeded in learning to read and write. In accomplishing this, I was compelled to resort to various stratagems. I had no regular teacher. My mistress, who had kindly commenced to instruct me, had, in compliance with the advice and direction of her husband, not only ceased to instruct, but had set her face against my being instructed by any one else. It is due, however, to my mistress to say of her, that she did not adopt this course of treatment immediately. She at first lacked the depravity indispensable to shutting me up in mental darkness. It was at least necessary for her to have some training in the exercise of irresponsible power, to make her equal to the task of treating me as though I were a brute.

My mistress was, as I have said, a kind and tender-hearted woman; and in the simplicity of her soul she commenced, when I first went to live with her, to treat me as she supposed one human being ought to treat another. In entering upon the duties of a slaveholder, she did not seem to perceive that I sustained to her the relation of a mere chattel, and that for her to treat me as a human being was not only wrong, but dangerously so. Slavery proved as injurious to her as it did to me. When I went there, she was a pious, warm, and tender-hearted woman. There was no sorrow or suffering for which she had not a tear. She had bread for the hungry, clothes for the naked, and comfort for every mourner that came within her reach. Slavery soon proved its ability to divest her of these heavenly qualities. Under its influence, the tender heart became stone, and the lamblike disposition gave way to one of tiger-like fierceness. The first step in her downward course was in her ceasing to instruct me. She now commenced to practise her husband's precepts. She finally became even more violent in her opposition than her husband himself. She was not satisfied with simply doing as well as he had commanded; she seemed anxious to do better. Nothing seemed to make her more angry than to see me with a newspaper. She seemed to think that here lay the danger. I have had her rush at me with a face made all up of fury and snatch from me a newspaper, in a manner that fully revealed her apprehension. She was an apt woman, and a little experience soon demonstrated, to her satisfaction, that education and slavery were incompatible with each other.

From this time I was most narrowly watched. If I was in a separate room any considerable length of time, I was sure to be suspected of having a book, and was at once called to give account of myself. All this, however, was too late. The first step had been taken. Mistress, in teaching me the alphabet, had given me the *inch,* and no precaution could prevent me from taking the *ell.*

The plan which I adopted, and the one by which I was most successful, was that of making friends of all the little white boys whom I met in the street. As many of these as I could, I converted into teachers. With their kindly aid, obtained at different times and in different places, I finally succeeded in learning to read. When I was sent [on] errands. I always took my book with me, and by going one part of my errand quickly, I found time to get a lesson before my return. I used also to carry bread with me, enough of which was always in the house, and to which I was always welcome; for I was much better off in this regard than many of the poor white children in our neighborhood. This bread I used to bestow upon the hungry little urchins, who, in return, would give me that more valuable bread of knowledge. I am strongly tempted to give the names of two or three of those little boys, as a testimonial of the gratitude and affection I bear them; but prudence forbids;—not that it would injure me, but it might embarrass them; for it is almost an unpardonable offence to teach slaves to read in this Christian country. It is enough to say of the dear little fellows, that they lived on Philpot Street, very near Durgin and Bailey's ship-yard. I used to talk this matter of slavery over with them. I would sometimes say to them, I wish I could be as free as they would be when they got to be men. "You will be free as soon as you are twenty-one, *but I am a slave for life!* Have not I as good a right to be free as you have?" These words used to trouble them; they would express for me the liveliest sympathy, and console me with the hope that something would occur by which I might be free.

Frederick Douglass became one of the most outspoken opponents of slavery. He was willing and able to describe the appalling details of slavery. But if he had possessed the passion to express himself, he had not acquired and mastered the reading, speaking, and writing skills for doing so effectively, his ability to communicate would have been weakened by lack of education. So it is with this in mind that one should view the importance of Frederick Douglass's clear understanding of the power of literacy. He understood as a child that freedom begins with knowledge, that slavery and knowledge are incompatible. And the question we may well ask ourselves as America enters the twenty-first century is, When we choose not to learn to read and write effectively, are we volunteering to be slaves?

SELECTED READINGS

Curry, George E., and Cornel West. 1996. *The Affirmative Action Debate.* Reading, Mass.: Addison Wesley.

Douglass, Frederick. Edited by Houston A. Baker. 1982. *Narrative of the Life of Frederick Douglass.* New York: Penguin Books.

Hamilton, Virginia. 1993. *Many Thousand Gone: African Americans from Slavery to Freedom.* New York: Random House, Incorporated.

Hutchinson, Earl Ofari. 1996. *The Assassination of The Black Male Image.* New York: Simon & Schuster.

Name _____   Date _____/_____/_____

QUESTIONS

1. *What was Frederick Douglass's purpose in learning to read? Did he understand the consequences when he made up his mind to learn to read? How important is understanding the consequences of your choices, when you are making commitments to plans and setting goals?*

2. *How did Frederick Douglass find himself a support system? How important is a support system when you are trying to reach a goal?*

3. *Define the word* ingenuity; *then tell how Frederick Douglass used ingenuity when learning to read. How important is personal initiative in helping you accomplish your goals? Explain.*

4 *Explain the term* volunteer slavery *and give some illustrations of how it might be occurring in our communities. List five "power points" (strategies or skills) you have learned from this chapter. List ways they can help a community combat modern forms of American slavery.*

5 *Make a list of the attitudes and habits that are detrimental to your well-being. Then, in small groups of two or three, see if one another's negative habits or attitudes are similar. Together, develop strategies for overcoming them.*

Berry Gordy (1929–)

Creative artist, founder of Motown Records and Motown Sound

"I Hear a Symphony"

There is something magical about this man. Berry Gordy can always sweet-talk an audience and conjure up a tune. There's a twinkle in his eye and warmth in his smile. He is a gentle man who at an early age grasped the concept of destiny. An observer of the human condition, he is not just a watcher of life's pantomines, viewing them through a daydreamer's microscope or a stargazer's telescope. You could call him an astroartist, though: one who drew an all-star cast of players from the musical worlds of urban America. They hitched a ride to a rhythm world where Berry Gordy was the star and the sky was his goal and a music-loving universe his limit. With genuine lyrical genius, he affirms that dreams do come true and that when you *share* your dream vision, the world will sing "I hear a symphony!"

Berry Gordy, founder and former CEO of Motown Records, may have influenced America's music industry more than anyone else in the history of this nation. As a young boy Berry watched the ebbing spirit in the lives of many fascinating members of his childhood community in Detroit's east side. If they had been born forty years later, these innovative, charismatic characters would have been university professors, lawyers, doctors, entrepreneurs. But because America was unkind and often relentless in dooming them to subordinate lives, Berry witnessed and frequently learned from their successes and their failures.

Some of those people seemed like cultural Dinosaurs, destined for destruction; their only song was to be a swan song. At this impressionable time in his young life, he understood their motives, recorded their moves, and avoided their misses. He became aware that smart people were not just those who did well in school; a smart person could be a small businessman or even a young songwriter like himself. This was a guiding principle that he never forgot, as he listened to his own inner music. He was not just stepping to the sound of a different drummer; he was creating the symphony of his life—themes that guided every thought, plan, and goal of that musical pilgrimage.

In the following excerpts from his revealing, historic autobiography *To Be Loved,* Berry Gordy shares his insights into how and why he has pursued with such passion his first love: music. And as you listen to the music of his life, ask yourself what song is being played in your life. What beat are you stepping to? What lyrics and melodies create passion and desire in your spirit? Is it the rhythm of prestige and power that moves you? Does the rap of family and friends inspire you? Will you have the power to sing your song, not someone else's song? As you read and listen closely, the song of your life may be one of the things you hear.

At age twenty-two, Berry Gordy came to the conclusion that he needed additional musical training. He enrolled in a music class with the expectation of learning how to play the clarinet. Within three weeks, he was kicked out of the group because of his wise-cracking and clowning antics. This was a setback for the young Berry Gordy but it did not stop his star from rising. Matter of fact it was the beginning of the legacy.

For the next few months all I could think about was songwriting. I wrote about everything, license plates, the sky, people, love, paper clips, you name it. I was a writing fool. Ideas were coming to me from everywhere. Even in my dreams I would hear songs and think to myself, "I wish I could have written something as beautiful as that." Then I'd wake up and realize I *had* written it. It was *my* dream. Amazing! But I could seldom remember the actual songs and arrangements. All I could remember was that I loved it. It was wonderful and the feeling stayed with me.

(Years later I began to keep a tape recorder next to my bed for these late-night inspirations. Saving ideas would become one of my greatest passions.)

Berry Gordy discovered early in his musical career that rhythm and creative genius transcend race, gender,

and even culture. For a good idea is a good idea . . . and a great artist is a great artist, no matter what color "earth suit" he or she was born with.

I was surprised by the white man I saw through the double glass windows standing in the middle of the studio floor, directing the band. Eyes closed, he was gesturing to the musicians to slow the tempo while finding a real groove. He was good. A white man with that much rhythm? I was impressed. His name was George Goldner. . . .

"I heard you were a good writer," was the first thing George Goldner said.

"I am," I said, smiling.

After looking over a couple of my songs, he told me, "Not bad." He then asked what I thought made a great record.

"Many things," I said.

"Like what?"

"Well, first of all, the song should be honest and have a good concept. The performance is important but the song's got to be sayin' something."

"Oh, is that so?"

"Probably the first thing people relate to is the melody, which includes hooks—phrases of repetition," I went on. "If that hook is infectious it's usually a hit. If it's monotonous, usually not."

George nodded slowly. He was impressed. "Got any money?"

"What's that?"

He pulled out a hundred dollar bill and gave it to me.

"It's like a down payment in case we ever do any business together." Then he left.

Wow! My ideas had translated into quick cash, ideas I felt I had a limitless supply of. I left that day in high spirits. It was more that just the hundred dollars. Here was a perfect stranger who saw value in my creative ideas. . . .

Though I would go on to have many exciting times in my life, the release of our first record with Jackie Wilson ranks among the top. . . . The excitement gave me a headache. My dream had come true. I was a hit songwriter. My troubles were over forever. I'd be rich! All the girls I ever wanted would now want me!

Then a feeling of anger started coming over me. All those people who said I'd "never be nothing" would now have to eat their words. Getting madder by the minute I started thinking how I was going to get even with everybody who had ever doubted me or treated me bad.

Wait a minute! What are you doing? You'd just better be happy and thankful for your own good fortune and not try to get back at anybody. After all, you're a star now and you better act like one.

I had given myself some good advice. I must admit though, that moment of anger felt pretty good.

I hadn't yet named it as such, but my *Cycle of Success* had just begun. Through the years, I would come to recognize and probe this most powerful pattern. When someone—anyone—becomes a star, his or her life goes through multiple changes brought on by fame, fortune, and power.

Very few can survive this vicious Cycle. People treat you differently. You treat people differently. You have newfound friends, newfound relatives, newfound business deals, newfound everything. You're expected to pay for things you've never had to pay for before. . . .

The Cycle has many aspects. When you feel like a star, you act and spend like one, racking up bills you can't afford.

In my case I had to keep up a front—that of a hot and happening songwriter. I had no clue how much money I was going to make, I just felt with a big hit I'd automatically be rich. Whenever I went out to bars or clubs, others would expect me to pick up the tab. I did. . . .

The Cycle has some good sides, too. I was so inspired that the sky became not the limit but just the first goal."

Berry Gordy began to crystalize his ideas into concrete realities. His Cycle of Success went into a new phase with the founding and development of Motown Records. He aimed Motown Records high above the multitude of mundane stargazers, and it soared like a powerful starship into unexplored galaxies. The Motown starship, in its celestial voyage, discovered a wellspring of new, bright, blazing stars whose legacy still burns as brilliantly as on the day they were discovered: raw, mysterious, magical.

. . .

As other independent record companies were failing, we were thriving. I am often asked, "How did you do it? How did you make it work at a time when so many barriers existed for black people and black music?" There are many answers to those questions but at the base of them is atmosphere. Hitsville [Motown] had an atmosphere that allowed people to experiment creatively and gave them the courage not to be afraid to make mistakes. In fact, I sometimes encouraged

mistakes. Everything starts as an idea and as far as I was concerned there were no stupid ones. "Stupid" ideas are what created the lightbulb, airplanes and the like. I never wanted people to feel how I felt in school—dumb. It was an atmosphere that made you feel no matter how high your goals, they were reachable, no matter who you were.

I had always figured that less than 1 percent of all the people in the world reach their full potential. Seeing that potential in others, I realized that by helping them reach theirs, maybe I could reach mine.

SELECTED READINGS

Fraser, George, and Les Brown. 1994. *Success Runs in Our Race: The Complete Guide to Effective Networking in the African American Community.* New York: William Morrow & Company, Incorporated.

Gawain, Shakti. 1982. *Creative Visualization.* New York: Bantam Books, Incorporated.

Gordy, Berry. 1994. *To Be Loved.* New York: Warner Books.

Monrow, Sylvester, and Peter Goldman. 1989. *Brothers: Black & Poor, A True Story of Courage and Survival.* New York: Ballantine Books, Incorporated.

Name _____ Date _____/_____/_____

QUESTIONS

1 *Have you ever felt that your ideas were stupid—and then, when you shared them with others, everyone seemed to think they were great ideas? How did you feel when this happened? What did you learn about yourself? Explain.*

2 *Why do you think Berry Gordy sees success as a cycle? Do you think success is a cyclic series of ups and downs? How important is understanding the Cycle of Success? Do you have a strategy for a Cycle of Success? Explain.*

3 *Have you ever had negative role models that you learned from? Explain what you learned and how it helped you avoid some pitfalls.*

4 *What human qualities do you think Berry Gordy admires? What human qualities do you admire?*

5 *How important is the principle of helping others reach their potential? Have you ever applied that principle in your life?*

Mae Carol Jemison
(1956–)

First African-American female astronaut

Higher than Hope

She has flown higher than most because she dared to aim higher than most. Dr. Mae Carol Jemison, the first African-American female astronaut, was born on October 17, 1956, in Decatur, Alabama, to Charlie and Dorothy Jemison. At the age of three, Mae moved with her family to Chicago to take advantage of better educational opportunities. Charlie, a custodian and Dorothy, a teacher always enjoyed a respect for education and instilled in their three children the curiosity and desire for learning. Mae was only four years old when an uncle who was a well known social worker with a love for science ignited in her a burning interest in the sciences.

Long before she ever stepped into a space capsule, she had become fascinated with learning, and this intense love of learning became the basis for her future. Exploring the various branches of science, whether astronomy, biology, or anthropology, became her chief interest in life.

At the library, Mae began reading to "navigate" the galaxies of scientific knowledge, exploring them at warp speed. Countless hours in the library did not sidetrack Mae from her other loves, dance and the arts, which were also a valued part of her life. Even though science was her focal point she felt that it should not consume her other interests. Determined to take an open-minded approach to learning, she pursued a variety of educational opportunities.

Mae used a selective strategy as she planned her college education: she would pursue a double major at Stanford University, earning degrees in chemical engineering (BS) and African-American studies (AB). This astute approach not only prepared her in the sciences but also opened doors to a clearer understanding of African-American history and of multiculturalism. She then attended Cornell University Medical College where she received her medical degree in 1981. Mae's medical training completed, she decided to put her skills to use in developing countries.

Mae traveled and performed medical services in such countries as Thailand, Sierra Leone, Liberia, and Kenya. In those different environments, she worked with doctors, other medical practitioners, and volunteers. She saw and absorbed much about those countries' cultural and medical practices, saw ancient healing techniques used in conjunction with modern medical science. The multicultural experiences gave her a unique perception and understanding of different parts of the world. They also deepened her appreciation of the medical care offered in the United States.

Mae Jemison's Third World exploits strengthened her belief that the best learning experiences for her should involve diverse interests and challenges. In October 1985, she applied to the National Aeronautics Space Administration (NASA) for a position in the space program. Two years later, NASA accepted her as an astronaut trainee in the most elite, most prestigious program in America—and possibly in the world. She completed the rigorous training and evaluations successfully within one year and became qualified as a mission specialist. However, it was not until September 12, 1992, that she stepped aboard the space shuttle *Endeavor* and was launched into space history as the first African-American female astronaut.

Several centuries earlier, African women had arrived in the Americas on slave ships. Now, one of their descendants was flying aboard a spaceship, exploring frontiers that most men and women in previous generations had never dreamed existed. A spirit of fearlessness and a desire to know carried Mae Jemison beyond the gravitational pull of doubt and uncertainty, as did the mind of a seeker and the heart of an adventurer. All her life, she had been ready to discover, to investigate, to explore the mysteries beyond the veil of the unknown. It was now that she "slipped the surly bonds of earth."

We know it isn't easy to explore any "unknown." Nor is it always easy to trade old habits for new, to change one career for another, to switch from one course to another course or change from one major to a different field. Creative change, though, needn't

be drastic or big. It can be a small change—which isn't necessarily a small thing. It can consist of meeting small incremental goals that lead to great change in our lives.

We can start "exploring"—implementing change—by planning differently, studying differently, reaching out to others differently, and just accepting ourselves differently. Reflecting on the story you've just read, you can readily see that Mae Jemison possessed an invaluable ability to stretch and grow. By embracing academic, artistic, and cultural challenges, she embraced creative change.

Creative change is always necessary for success. It is impossible to explore the frontiers of our own potential unless we are willing to embrace the challenges of creative change. We *must* be ever ready to creatively change our minds, our goals, even our associates, for positive development and growth.

Change, however, must not become an excuse for running from problems or from the things we fear. Neither should change become an excuse for lack of commitment and follow-through. Learning, discovering, and exploring through creative change should become a joyful, insatiable adventure. Thus, we must continue to assimilate creative change and vision into our lives, keep our minds open to fresh, new approaches to thinking and acting. We should not, of course, abandon old ways simply because they are old, yet we must not stay attached to them merely because they feel comfortable and easy.

Mae Jemison's life exhibits the gift of knowing when to seize an opportunity. Opportunity comes in many forms, and all too many people tend to be unaware of it. Try to develop an eye for open doors! And when those opportunities come, be ready to seize them.

SELECTED READINGS

Beckham, Barry. 1984. *The Black Student's Guide to Colleges.* Hampton, Va.: Beckham House Publishers.

Bunkley, Crawford B. 1996. *The African-American Network.* New York: Plume Publishers.

Lyles, Charlise. 1994. *Do I Dare Disturb the Universe? From the Projects to Prep School.* London: Faber and Faber, Incorporated.

Potter, Joan, with Constance Claytor and Alison Munoz (illustrator). 1994. *African-American Firsts.* Elizabethtown, N.Y.: Pinto Press.

Questions

1   *If you have experienced living with or visiting members of other cultures, how did you view those people and how did they view you?*

2   *What country or culture would you like to visit? At the library, locate information about it. Have you considered study in another country for a year? If so, which country and why?*

3   *How important is having diverse experiences in understanding people of different backgrounds? Do you have any friends from different cultures? How did you meet and what did you have in common?*

4   *Why would you consider Mae Jemison a positive role model? If you met her, what would you like her to tell you about her space travel?*

5   *Why does this essay refer to her as fearless? Do you consider fearlessness essential to success? Explain the difference between fearlessness and recklessness.*

Reginald Lewis (1942–1993)

Chief Executive Officer, 1987–1993, of TLC Beatrice, one of the largest African-American-owned businesses today

Roots and Wings

Provocative, irascible, and ambitious, Reginald Lewis was a mystery to many and a towering icon to knowledgeable African-American entrepreneurs. He was born December 7, 1942, to Clinton and Carolyn Lewis. His birth occurred on the first day of World War II. He was not a man who could be pigeonholed, passed by, or forgotten. Once you met Reginald Lewis, his bewitching personality seemed literally burned into your consciousness. His deep piercing eyes and his physical prowess always demanded respect. Even as a young boy growing up in the blue collar, working class neighborhood of East Baltimore, his very presence said that he was somebody.

Very shortly after Reginald's birth, Carolyn and Clinton Lewis separated. Reggie and his mother moved into her parents' home. It was there that Reginald Lewis gained an understanding of his roots and it was there that he received his wings. It was there that Reggie learned the value of hard work and it was there that he also learned the value of great dreams.

I remember being in the bathtub, and my grandmother and grandfather were talking about some incident that had been unfair and was racial in nature. They were talking about work and accomplishing things and how racism was getting in the way of that. And they looked at me and said, "Well, maybe it will be different for him."

I couldn't have been more than six years old.

One of them, I can't remember whether it was my grandfather or my grandmother, said to me, "Well, is it going to be any different for you?"

And as I was climbing out of the tub and they were putting a towel around me, I looked up and said, "Yeah, cause why should white guys have all the fun?"

Young Reggie Lewis grew up to be a remarkable man, one who understood his purpose and his season. He came to realize that a triumphant life is not static, but progressive, and no one has forever to reach personal goals. So with a single-minded, clear-cut focus, he grasped the opportunities that led to his destiny. No natural, artificial, or imaginable obstacle would stand in his way, for this man of grace, courage, and determination was meant to do great things.

My mother left my father when I was 5 and arrived at grandma's house in the middle of the night with me under her arm. Everybody got out of bed. Grandmom and Grandpop, Aunts Charlotte, Beverly, Jean, and Elaine, Uncles James and Donald. Uncle Sam was away in college. Aunt Doris was married and Uncle Robert was in the Air Force. After my grandfather exploded about more mouths to feed, Grandmom asked one of my aunts to take me up to bed. As I went upstairs, I heard my mother say that we would not be a burden, we'd pay our way. That stuck."

The lesson he learned that night was one that Reginald Lewis would carry with him all his life. He would also have, in years to come, very fond memories of living with his grandparents. He remembered them—Sam and Sue Cooper—as wise beyond any formal education. They taught him to have a gentleman's demeanor, but a warrior's heart, a principle he applied and practiced in courtrooms and in some of America's largest corporate boardrooms. He reflected on his grandparents' outlook when he had children of his own:

I feel very good about my base values, which I think . . . so important that we instill in our young people and children. On this note I think of my grandparents, even more than my mother. My mother was active, having a lot of other children and dealing with all that entails. But my grandparents, I think, had a wonderful facility for programming young people. And being able to convince you that you were someone special, that you had something to bring or something to contribute, too.

I carried that with me a long way. It's been extremely important to me.

Thanks to the Cooper family, I never had a fear of white people. And I think my grandmother always emphasized, "Don't be afraid of them. Be afraid of situations or be

concerned in certain situations, but never fear any person—be they black or white." And she never showed any fear in terms of dealing with whites. And that was important, because that wasn't true with a lot of other people that I've known.

. . .

[At Dunbar High School] I was accepted into the "in crowd" right away because of my ability in sports. . . . In all modesty, I was a hell of a performer. I earned four varsity letters in baseball, three in football—where I was the starting quarterback from my sophomore year on, and two varsity letters in basketball. In football, I believed there were only two passers in Maryland worthy of mention—Johnny Unitas and me. I could put the ball on a dime from 40 yards. And when I played, I never doubted my ability and could look into the eyes of my teammates when the heat was really on and tell who could perform and who couldn't.

I also learned that the voice and the eyes in the huddle could make a real difference. When you said, "Okay, we're going in," you had to mean it and you had to deliver. I generally had a reputation that I came to play and that I was serious about the game.

As a result of Reggie Lewis's athletic achievements, he received an athletic scholarship to Virginia State College to play football for four years. Reggie had difficulty adjusting to the academic rigors of the freshman year, especially in mathematics, and lost his football scholarship. He even received an incomplete in a freshman orientation class that he had refused to attend. A change of attitude in his sophomore year resulted in better grades; mathematics, however, continued to be a thorn in his side. Years later, Reggie Lewis would establish a $5,000 stipend for Virginia State seniors who had the highest cumulative average in mathematics. Here are some of his comments about his college years:

I quit football after my freshman year and decided to get serious about my studies. The college years were wild. I crammed a lot of living into those four years. After a rotten freshman year, I really started to study. I got straight A's in economics and always went beyond the course. I started reading the *New York Times* and [the] *Wall Street Journal* every day. But I had fun, too. . . .

I began to think about graduate school or law school or maybe, just maybe, a really great university like Harvard. . . .

In my senior year, lightning struck. Harvard Law School started a program to select a few black students to attend summer school at Harvard, to introduce them to legal study in general. Participating colleges would select five students from their respective schools and Harvard Law School would select just one student from each school.

I was excited, I mean, really excited. Calm down, calm down, I told myself. Develop a plan. It wasn't easy knowing where to begin. First, I needed to get the literature on the program. My school only gave a summary of it, so I wrote Harvard for specific details the same day I found out about the program. Harvard responded immediately, which really impressed me. My approach was to make sure I was selected by Virginia State. That would not be easy. Many students had straight A's and I had had a rotten freshman year, which hurt my cumulative grade point average.

I needed to supplement my application—obtain letters of recommendation perhaps. I spoke to a couple of professors. I told them that this was my big shot at the big time. I said I didn't want a letter that just said "he's a nice guy," but a real substantive letter setting out what I did well and what I did poorly. I gave them a biography, grades, and everything. . . .

Well, I made the college list, fifth. The college recommended four people above me because their cumulative averages were higher. But I made the cut. OK! . . .

Then the letter came—I was going to Harvard for the summer. I later learned that Harvard discredited my freshman year and liked my straight A's in economics and the letter of recommendation. The night I got the letter, I told my roommate, Alan Colon, "Alan, come September I will be in the incoming class at Harvard Law." He said, "Reg, this is just for the summer. Don't get yourself up for a major disappointment." I said, "Alan, just watch—I'm going to Harvard."

Reggie Lewis was not a young man who made statements he wouldn't be able to confirm, to follow through on. When he said he was going to Harvard, he meant it. Now it was just a matter of how to get there:

I needed a plan. An incredible calm came over me and the plan began to emerge. First, have a tremendous final year in college; second, know the objectives of the program; third, break your [butt] over the summer, eliminate all distractions—nothing except the objective. The program was held over two four-week semesters: during the first semester,

say nothing about going to Harvard. First prove that you can compete, for example, take a difficult course at Harvard College during the summer and do well. Second, do the job. Build upon your strengths. This was the brief and I've never executed better.

The Harvard summer program opened, for Reginald Lewis, a door on a whole new world. Characteristically, though, he had kicked the door open, instead of waiting to be ushered in.

A funny thing happened during that summer. By the end of the program, I really didn't care whether I got in or not. I had done my best and I knew I could compete. I had given it my best shot. That was enough. IBM had offered me a job last spring in their office products division in Trenton, New Jersey. I also had a shot at the PhD program at Michigan. So I had alternatives. . . .

At a farewell banquet for all the participants in the summer program, Associate Dean Louis Toepfler told me that he would like me to call him at midweek. When I did, Toepfler's secretary asked if I would speak to her, since the Dean was not in. She had before her a letter she was in the process of typing to me. I said of course. The opening line was, "There will be a place for you in this fall's class, if you want it." Great news! Plus the school was making loans available and gave me a one-year grant from the Rockefeller Foundation.

Harvard's generosity made a lasting impact on the young man. Later, he would repay Harvard many times over. In 1992, he gave Harvard Law School a $3 million gift—at the time, the largest gift in the school's history. In gratitude the law school named its international law building the Reginald F. Lewis International Center. It was the first building on campus to be named for an African American.

After graduating from Harvard law school, Reginald Lewis landed a job with a hot New York law firm, Paul, Weiss, Rifkind, Wharton & Garrison. There he was assigned to the busy corporate law department where young lawyers could sharpen their corporate skills. He did the fundamental work of preparing joint ventures, setting up corporations and filing securities. After two years practicing law he was ready to do his own thing. Reginald Lewis started his own law firm. The firm was one of the first African-American law firms on Wall Street. Through the dynamic leadership of Lewis, the firm prospered and within a short period of time his client list included such notables as the Ford Foundation, Equitable Life, and General Foods. Reginald Lewis's negotiating skills had become a standard of excellence in the Wall Street community. But Reggie was not satisfied, he wanted to fry bigger fish. He wanted to become an owner and run his own company. In 1975, he tried to acquire Park Sausages, a small company in Baltimore, Maryland. The acquisition of the company did not occur but he gained a lot of respect and credibility as a serious buyer in search of a company. On January 29, 1984, Reginald Lewis made his first major acquisition with the purchase of McCall Pattern Company. Reginald Lewis had arrived; he was now the owner of a company that had 580 employees and an annual revenue of $51,000,000. He had learned the buy out game well and would use his expertise to increase his wealth and satisfy his ambitions for business. On August 6, 1987, after 19 years of courtrooms, boardrooms, meetings, and negotiations, Reginald Lewis signed an agreement to purchase Beatrice for $985,000,000.

In 1987, Reginald Lewis purchased TLC Beatrice. Beatrice became one of the largest African-American owned businesses in America, with annual sales of over one billion dollars. His company owned subsidiaries in over thirty-one countries throughout the world. His philanthropic endowments are legendary within the African-American educational, charitable, and business communities. After a battle with brain cancer, Lewis died in 1993, leaving a legacy of success.

Source: From *Why Should White Guys Have All the Fun?* by Reggie Lewis. Copyright © 1994. Reprinted by permission of John Wiley & Sons, Inc.

SELECTED READINGS

Boston, Kelvin, and Dennis Kimbro. 1996. *Smart Money Moves for African Americans.* New York: The Putnam Publishing Group.

Kunjufu, Jawanza. 1996. *Restoring the Village, Values, and Commitment: Solutions for the Black Family.* Chicago: African American Images.

Lewis, Reggie. 1995. *Why Should White Guys Have All the Fun.* New York: John Wiley & Sons.

Vanzant, Iyanla. 1996. *The Spirit of a Man: A Vision of Transformation for Black Men and the Women Who Love Them.* San Francisco: Harper San Francisco.

Name _____   Date _____/_____/_____

QUESTIONS

1 Investigate and see how many African Americans you can find who were as successful in business as Reginald Lewis. Compare and contrast how they made their fortunes. What kind of knowledge and characteristics do you think a person must have, to own and develop a billion-dollar business?

2 How did the values that Reggie's grandparents taught him influence his attitude toward success?

3 How important was planning to Reggie Lewis when he first considered attending Harvard University? How important is planning in your life? Have you begun to develop your plan for achievement?

4 *What are the benefits of planning for success? What kind of attitude did Reginald Lewis have about academic competition? What was his attitude about doing one's best? What is your own?*

5 *Why is it important to give back to the community that supports your efforts? Have you considered ways to give back to the community that supports your attempts to be successful? Explain.*

Nelson R. Mandela
(1918–)

President of the Republic of South Africa since 1994; freedom fighter

Many More Hills to Climb

The title African-American profiles would lead one to conclude that the persons who have been highlighted in this text are all African Americans. Then why include Nelson Mandela, a freedom fighter and Nobel Peace Prize recipient? Nelson Mandela is a man whose life transcends race, culture, and politics. Many African Americans marched for his release from prison, cried for his family, and prayed for his victory. His struggle and victory against apartheid have been the rallying point for many African Americans. It is with this spirit of unity that we include Nelson Mandela among the courageous African Americans featured in this text.

Amandla, amandla [power, power]! roared the crowd, as Nelson R. Mandela stepped confidently toward the podium to be sworn in as the first president of the new Republic of South Africa. One of the most highly admired men of the twentieth century, he had spent almost eight decades under the old South African segregation system of apartheid.

Apartheid was one of the most racially oppressive and degrading systems in the history of humanity. Mandela's opposition to apartheid and his commitment to freedom had cost him almost thirty years of his life—years spent in prison. His struggle exemplified total devotion to and sacrifice for the democratic principle that all human beings are created equal.

Mandela's long road to freedom had many detours and delays. There were challenges looming like mountains that had to be climbed, and valleys of sadness and loneliness that had to be traversed and endured. Sometimes the sacrifices, the deaths, the long periods of separation from family and friends seemed too great a price to pay. Yet in reality, the cost of freedom is always high, a price that free people must appreciate and always be willing to pay.

His journey was a remarkably courageous undertaking. It was a journey of patience with resistance. It was a journey of small steps taken with a giant hope, a hope that never faltered or grew faint, a hope that, step by step, lifted him from oppression to leadership, to resistance, to endurance, to freedom, to inauguration as president of South Africa. It was, quite simply, a feat unequaled anywhere else during the twentieth century.

In the following essay, Mandela reflects soberly on this momentous accomplishment. He does so with the slow and deliberate wisdom of a seasoned soldier who savors the victory but will always remember the cost. Success always has a cost. As you read and think about this freedom fighter's journey from the wilderness of apartheid to the promised land of democracy, ask yourself: Am I willing to pay the cost of success?

May 10 dawned bright and clear. For the past few days, I had been pleasantly besieged by arriving dignitaries and world leaders who were coming to pay their respects before the inauguration. The inauguration would be the largest gathering ever of international leaders on South African soil.

The ceremonies took place in the lovely sandstone amphitheater formed by the Union Building in Pretoria. For decades, this had been the seat of white supremacy, and now it was the site of a rainbow gathering of different colors and nations for the installation of South Africa's first democratic, nonracial government.

On that lovely autumn day I was accompanied by my daughter Zenani. On the podium, Mr. de Klerk [former president of the Republic of South Africa] was first sworn in as second deputy president. Then Thabo Mbeki was sworn in as first deputy president. When it was my turn, I pledged to obey and uphold the constitution and to devote myself to the well-being of the republic and its people. To the assembled guests and the watching world, I said:

"Today, all of us do, by our presence here . . . confer glory and hope to newborn liberty. Out of the experience of an extraordinary human disaster that lasted too long, must be born a society of which all humanity will be proud.

". . . We, who were outlaws not so long ago, have today been given the rare privilege to be host to the nations of the world on our own soil. We thank all of our distinguished international guests for having come to take possession with

the people of our country of what is, after all, a common victory for justice, for peace, for human dignity.

"We have, at last, achieved our political emancipation. We pledge ourselves to liberate all our people from the continuing bondage of poverty, deprivation, suffering, gender, and other discrimination.

"Never, never, and never again shall it be that this beautiful land will again experience the oppression of one by another. . . . The sun shall never set on so glorious a human achievement.

"Let freedom reign. God bless Africa!"

A few moments later we all lifted our eyes in awe as a spectacular array of South African jets, helicopters, and troop carriers roared in perfect formation over the Union Buildings. It was not only a display of pinpoint precision and military force, but a demonstration of the military's loyalty to democracy, to a new government that had been freely and fairly elected. Only moments before, the highest generals of the South African Defense Force and police, their chests bedecked with ribbons and medals from days gone by, saluted me and pledged their loyalty. I was not unmindful of the fact that not so many years before they would not have saluted but arrested me. Finally a chevron of Impala jets left a smoke trail of the black, red, green, blue, white, and gold of the new South Africa flag.

The day was symbolized for me by the playing of our two national anthems, and the vision of whites singing "*Nkosi Sikelel' iAfrika*" [God Bless Africa] and blacks singing "*Die Stem* [van Suid Afrika]," [The Call of South Africa] the old anthem of the republic. Although that day, neither group knew the lyrics of the anthem they once despised, they would soon know the words by heart.

On the day of the inauguration, I was overwhelmed with a sense of history. In the first decade of the twentieth century, a few years after the bitter Anglo-Boer War and before my own birth, the white-skinned peoples of South Africa patched up their differences and erected a system of racial domination against the dark-skinned peoples of their own land. The structure they created formed the basis of one of the harshest, most inhumane societies the world has ever known. Now, in the last decade of the twentieth century, and my own eighth decade as a man, that system had been overturned forever and replaced by one that recognized the rights and freedoms of all peoples regardless of the color of their skin.

That day had come about through the unimaginable sacrifices of thousands of my people, people whose suffering and courage can never be counted or repaid. I felt that day, as I have on so many other days, that I was simply the sum of all those African patriots who had gone before me. That long and noble line ended and now began again with me. I was pained that I was not able to thank them and that they were not able to see what their sacrifices had wrought.

The policy of apartheid created a deep and lasting wound in my country and my people. All of us will spend many years, if not generations, recovering from that profound hurt. But the decades of oppression and brutality had another, unintended effect, and that was that it produced the Oliver Tambos, the Walter Sisulus, the Chief Luthulis, the Yusuf Dadoos, the Bram Fischers, the Robert Sobukwes of our time—men of such extraordinary courage, wisdom, and generosity that their like may never be known again. Perhaps it requires such depth of oppression to create such heights of character. My country is rich in the minerals and gems that lie beneath its soil, but I have always known that its greatest wealth is its people, finer and truer than the purest diamonds.

It is from these comrades in the struggle that I learned the meaning of courage. Time and again, I have seen men and women risk and give their lives for an idea. I have seen men stand up to attacks and torture without breaking, showing a strength and resiliency that defies the imagination. I learned that courage was not the absence of fear, but the triumph over it. I felt fear myself more times than I can remember, but I hid it behind a mask of boldness. The brave man is not he who does not feel afraid, but he who conquers that fear.

I never lost hope that this great transformation would occur. Not only because of the great heroes I have already cited, but because of the courage of the ordinary men and women of my country. I always knew that deep down in every human heart, there is mercy and generosity. No one is born hating another person because of the color of his skin, or his background, or his religion. People must learn to hate, and if they can learn to hate, they can be taught to love, for love comes more naturally to the human heart than its opposite. Even in the grimmest times in prison, when my comrades and I were pushed to our limits, I would see a glimmer of humanity in one of the guards, perhaps just for a second, but it was enough to reassure me and keep me going. Man's goodness is a flame that can be hidden but never extinguished.

We took up the struggle with our eyes wide open, under no illusion that the path would be an easy one. As a young man, when I joined the African National Congress, I saw the price my comrades paid for their beliefs, and it was high. For myself, I have never regretted my commitment to the struggle, and I was always prepared to face the hardships that

affected me personally. But my family paid a terrible price, perhaps too dear a price for my commitment.

In life, every man has twin obligations—obligations to his family, to his parents, to his wife and children; and he has an obligation to his people, his community, his country. In a civil and humane society, each man is able to fulfill those obligations according to his own inclinations and abilities. But in a country like South Africa, it was almost impossible for a man of my birth and color to fulfill both of those obligations. In South Africa, a man of color who attempted to live as a human being was punished and isolated. In South Africa, a man who tried to fulfill his duty to his people was inevitably ripped from his family and his home and was forced to live a life apart, a twilight existence of secrecy and rebellion. I did not in the beginning choose to place my people above my family, but in attempting to serve my people, I found that I was prevented from fulfilling my obligations as a son, a brother, a father, and a husband.

In that way, my commitment to my people, to the millions of South Africans I would never know or meet, was at the expense of the people I knew best and loved most. It was as simple and yet as incomprehensible as the moment a small child asks her father, "Why can you not be with us?" And the father must utter the terrible words: "There are other children like you, a great many of them . . ." and then one's voice trails off.

I was not born with a hunger to be free. I was born free—free in every way that I could know. Free to run in the fields near my mother's hut, free to swim in the clear stream that ran through my village, free to roast mealies under the stars and ride the broad backs of slow-moving bulls. As long as I obeyed my father and abided by the customs of my tribe, I was not troubled by the laws of man or God.

It was only when I began to learn that my boyhood freedom was an illusion, when I discovered as a young man that my freedom had already been taken from me, that I began to hunger for it. At first, as a student, I wanted freedom only for myself, the transitory freedoms of being able to stay out at night, read what I pleased, and go where I chose. Later, as a young man in Johannesburg, I yearned for the basic and honorable freedoms of achieving my potential, of earning my keep, of marrying and having a family—the freedom not to be obstructed in a lawful life.

But then I slowly saw that not only was I not free, but my brothers and sisters were not free. I saw that it was not just my freedom that was curtailed, but the freedom of everyone who looked like I did. That is when I joined the African National Congress, and that is when the hunger for my freedom became the greater hunger for the freedom of my people. It was this desire for the freedom of my people to live their lives with dignity and self-respect that animated my life, that transformed a frightened young man into a bold one, that drove a law-abiding attorney to become a criminal, that turned a family-loving husband into a man without a home, that forced a life-loving man to live like a monk. I am no more virtuous or self-sacrificing than the next man, but I found that I could not even enjoy the poor and limited freedoms I was allowed when I knew my people were not free. Freedom is indivisible; the chains on any one of my people were the chains on all of them, the chains on all of my people were the chains on me.

It was during those long and lonely years that my hunger for the freedom of my own people became a hunger for the freedom of all people, white and black. I knew as well as I knew anything that the oppressor must be liberated just as surely as the oppressed. A man who takes another man's freedom is a prisoner of hatred, he is locked behind the bars of prejudice and narrow-mindedness. I am not truly free if I am taking away someone else's freedom, just as surely as I am not free when my freedom is taken from me. The oppressed and the oppressor alike are robbed of their humanity.

When I walked out of prison, that was my mission, to liberate the oppressed and the oppressor both. Some say that has now been achieved. But I know that that is not the case. The truth is that we are not yet free; we have merely achieved the freedom to be free, the right not to be oppressed. We have not taken the final step of our journey, but the first step on a longer and even more difficult road. For to be free is not merely to cast off one's chains, but to live in a way that respects and enhances the freedom of others. The true test of our devotion to freedom is just beginning.

I have walked that long road to freedom. I have tried not to falter; I have made missteps along the way. But I have discovered the secret that after climbing a great hill, one only finds that there are many more hills to climb. I have taken a moment here to rest, to steal a view of the glorious vista that surrounds me, to look back on the distance I have come. But I can rest only for a moment, for with freedom comes responsibilities, and I dare not linger, for my long walk is not yet ended.

Kimbro, Dennis. 1993. *Daily Motivations for African-American Success.* New York: Fawcett Book Group.

Mandela, Nelson. 1986. *The Struggle Is My Life.* New York: Pathfinder Press.

Meer, Fatima. 1988. *Higher Than Hope.* New York: Harper & Row.

Name _____   Date _____/_____/_____

QUESTIONS

1 List the positive traits, or characteristics, that you think Nelson Mandela possessed and drew upon to accomplish his goal of dismantling the apartheid system.

2 Which of his positive traits do you admire most? List five people who possess it. Why does this trait seem so important to you? Explain.

3 Why is it important to understand that yesterday's achievements can become obsolete in regard to solving tomorrow's problems? If you have ever had money problems or scheduling problems, did you experience any shifts in your goals when you could not aim for or reach them as planned? List and discuss those changes. Then begin to develop a personal success journal, recording your goals, strategies, obstacles, and successes.

4 *Why is education a lifelong journey? Do you know anyone who returned to school after age fifty? Discuss with that person how school has changed since he or she last attended.*

5 *What does Mandela's life teach about staying focused on your goals, even when this appears to be a hopeless effort? Have you had an experience in which a goal looked hopeless? What did you do about the situation?*

Thurgood Marshall (1908–1993)

First African-American Associate Justice of the United States Supreme Court (1967–1991); lead attorney for the National Association for the Advancement of Colored People (1935–1962)

Rebel for Justice

Thurgood Marshall was a valiant warrior: not, perhaps, in the most literal sense, yet he was one of the greatest fighters for justice this country has ever known. He was determined to be nothing less than America's legal conscience. No matter how unseeing, rigid, or indifferent the judicial system might seem toward change, he stood steadfast for justice, righteousness, and truth for every citizen.

Biographer Michael D. Davis offers some significant background facts:

Thurgood Marshall was born July 2, 1908, in Baltimore, Maryland, in the Chesapeake Bay region that proclaims itself "The Land of Pleasant Living." It was a city where many white people remained proud of being south of the Mason-Dixon Line.

His maternal great-grandfather, a slave whose name the family never knew, was brought to America by slave traders during the 1840s and sold to a plantation owner on Maryland's Eastern Shore. Marshall said his great-grandfather came from the Congo, known as the Republic of Zaire since 1971: "His more polite descendants like to think he came from the cultured tribes in Sierra Leone, but we all know that he really came from the toughest part of the Congo."

In a *Time* magazine interview, Marshall described his great-grandfather as "one mean man." Elsewhere he characterized him proudly as the "baddest nigger" in Maryland. "One day his owner came up to him and said, 'Look, I brought you here so I guess I can't very well shoot you—as you deserve. On the other hand, I can't with a clear conscience sell anyone as vicious as you to another slaveholder, and I can't give you away. So, I am going to set you free—on one condition. Get the hell out of this county and never come back.'"

"That was the only time Massuh didn't get an argument from the old boy," Marshall added. Still defiant, his great-grandfather married a white woman and raised his family just a few miles from his former owner's plantation, living there until he died. . . .

Thurgood Marshall traced his family's history and name to Africa. The only name many slaves had was their owner's. Thurgood's paternal grandfather was a freedman—a former slave—known as Marshall. During the Civil War he joined a black regiment, one of 186,000 former slaves to fight with Union troops. Soldiers were required to have first and last names, so he took the first name Thoroughgood to comply with that regulation. "I was named after him," Marshall told an interviewer, "but by the time I was in second grade, I got tired of spelling all that and shortened it."

Thurgood loved to hear inspiring stories about his ancestors, stories that spoke of proud, rebellious, and free-spirited people. The more he heard, the more impressed he was with their ability to survive a system that treated them as less than human. And the more he heard, the more he wanted to know, for he had come to love his heritage.

In the same ancestral spirit of defiance, love of freedom, and independent thinking, Thurgood Marshall became thoroughly good at whatever he undertook. He continued the battle against oppressive "slave masters." It didn't matter whether they were dressed in white sheets, hiding bloodstained hands, or in black robes, bolstering limp white laws—laws that were drenched with black suffering, pain, and death. The American apartheid system was his enemy, racist tradition his nemesis, and injustice his chief opponent. His passion for and commitment to justice sustained him during some of the most trying phases of this country's history of segregation.

During the 1920s the choice of black students destined for college was limited. White southern colleges did not accept them. That was the law. Very few black students attended integrated schools in other parts of the United States. Thurgood applied to Lincoln University in Chester, Pennsylvania, the nation's oldest black college and his brother's alma mater. It had been founded in 1854 by a Presbyterian minister and his wife. Lincoln's charter called for "the scientific, classical and theological education of colored youth of the male sex. . . ."

One night Marshall went with a group of six fellow students to a movie in nearby Oxford. After they purchased their tickets, an usher reminded them that black patrons were

restricted to the balcony, commonly referred to as the "nosebleed section" or "nigger heaven." The students ignored the usher's admonition and took seats in the theater's whites-only orchestra. When the usher ordered them to move, they kept their seats, seemingly engrossed with the western movie. Thurgood recalled hearing a bitter voice in the theater's darkness saying, "Nigger, why don't you just get out of here and sit where you belong?"

Marshall told the man that he had paid for his ticket and did not intend to move from his comfortable orchestra seat. Recalling the incident in a letter to his parents, he wrote, "You can't really tell what a person like that looks like because it's just an ugly feeling that's looking at you, not a real face. We found out that they only had one fat cop in the whole town and they wouldn't have the nerve or the room in the jail to arrest all of us. But the amazing thing was that when we were leaving, we just walked out with all those other people and they didn't do anything, didn't say anything, didn't even look at us—at least, not as far as I know. I'm not sure I like being invisible, but maybe it's better than being put to shame and not able to respect yourself."

Thurgood said the Oxford movie theater incident started his civil rights career. "The leader of that group at Lincoln was a guy named U. S. Tate. He was the leader who said we ought to do something about it. We desegregated the theater in the little town of Oxford. I guess that's what started the whole thing in my life."

Moved by this incident in a small theater in a small town, Thurgood Marshall would never be the same again. Never again would he look at segregation with the same innocent eye, regardless of how small or insignificant the discrimination appeared. Having developed a large distaste for the fruits of segregation, he was more mature. Yes: there was something different about him now. . . .

In June 1930, after marrying Vivian Burey in his senior year, Thurgood Marshall received his bachelor's degree from Lincoln University. That same year, he applied to the University of Maryland law school. Thurgood had his life all planned. He would be living in Baltimore with his new wife; he would attend the university's law school at reduced cost because he was a resident of Maryland. He would graduate and then practice law in Baltimore. However, he was refused entry to the University of Maryland Law School because of its segregation policies.

In the meantime he applied for, and was quickly admitted to, Howard University's law school in Washington, D.C. . . . Marshall committed himself to the study of law and the twice-a-day forty-mile rides in segregated rail cars, reading law books all the way. It was a grueling schedule. During his first year in law school, Thurgood left Baltimore every weekday at 5:30 A.M., attended classes until 3:00 P.M., then returned to one of his part-time jobs as a waiter, a bellhop, and a baker at Preece's Bakery on Pennsylvania Avenue. Then he studied until midnight. "I heard law books were to dig in," he said, "so I dug deep. I got through simply by overwhelming the job, and I was at it twenty hours a day, seven days a week."

Despite the rigorous routine, during which the weight on his six-foot frame dropped from 170 to 130 pounds, law school proved a rewarding and challenging experience. Remembering his first week at Howard, he said, "This is what I wanted to do for as long as I lived." Thurgood said that he enjoyed the forensic debates and the verbal sparring that went along with his studies and that he believed his oratorical skills would be an asset in the practice of law.

In 1933, Thurgood Marshall graduated from law school first in his class, passed the Maryland state bar examination, and established a law practice in Baltimore. As in so many other cities throughout the United States, there were very few black lawyers there to represent the interests of black people. Thurgood was the people's lawyer, providing services to black people whether they were able to pay or not.

By 1938, after pleading all types of cases for poor, downtrodden, and forgotten African Americans in Baltimore, Thurgood became the chief counsel for the NAACP. He immediately moved to New York City to take charge of the organization's legal matters. In a moral sense, Thurgood Marshall became Black America's attorney general, as he began an all-out assault on the supposedly insurmountable doctrine of "separate but equal" arrangements for the blacks.

At the risk of his life, Marshall traveled throughout the United States, investigating lynchings, Klu Klux Klan activities, and injustices perpetrated upon powerless and innocent blacks. He was an eagle first soaring above, then attacking, the evils of ignorance, hate, and viciousness. He was a fearless and determined, "Thoroughgood" responding to his people's cry.

After decades of struggle, the NAACP, led by the legal expertise of Thurgood Marshall, assembled the finest possible team of legal minds to combat segregation. Lawyers and some of the best American social scientists of the time were brought in. Their every move was directed toward dismantling racial discrimination. An encounter on the battlefield of justice appeared imminent.

May 17, 1954, after endless hours of research, strategy sessions, and disappointments, the warrior's crescendo with its symphony of freedom and liberation was heard. It was the day that changed American education forever, Thurgood Marshall, a champion for justice, faced the Supreme Court of the United States. As the attorney for the NAACP, he had argued on behalf of the plaintiff, a school child named Linda Brown, in the landmark case *Brown* v. *Board of Education of Topeka*. Now he listened while a justice of the Court declared, "In the field of public education the doctrine of 'separate but equal' has no place. Separate educational facilities are inherently unequal." This was one of the greatest days in the history of the Supreme Court of this great land. This was the day that stood as a requiem for "Separate but Equal." For that day, the veil of segregation had tumbled down. American justice itself, along with Thurgood Marshall, stood a little taller.

Source: From *Thurgood Marshall: Warrior at the Bar, Rebel on the Bench* by Michael D. Davis and Hunter R. Clark. Copyright © 1992 by Michael D. Davis and Hunter R. Clark. Published by arrangement with Carol Publishing Group. A Birch Lane Press Book.

SELECTED READINGS

Brice, Carleen. 1994. *Walk Tall: Affirmations for People of Color.* San Diego: RPI Publishing, Incorporated.

Davis, Michael D., and Hunter R. Clark. 1992. *Thurgood Marshall: Warrior at the Bar, Rebel on the Bench.* New York: Carol Publishing Group.

Goldman, Roger, and David Gallen. 1992. *Thurgood Marshall: Justice for All.* New York: Caroll & Graff Publishers.

Kimbro, Dennis. 1997. *What Makes the Great: Strategies for Extraordinary Achievement.* New York: Doubleday and Company, Incorporated.

Name _____ Date _____/_____/_____

QUESTIONS

1 *Investigate your roots—your ethnic heritage. Do you think your roots have had or will have an influence in your life? How do you think Thurgood Marshall's understanding of his roots affected his success?*

2 *What do you think is the main message of this profile? Explain.*

3 *Is there an African American today whom you would compare to Thurgood Marshall? How are they similar? How are they different?*

4 *Research the case of* Brown v. Board of Education of Topeka *and write a summary of it. Then discuss how you think it influenced Thurgood Marshall's life.*

5 *How important is giving your talents to the community?*

Benjamin E. Mays
(1894–1984)
President of Morehouse College, 1941–1967

Never Accept Mediocrity as a Goal

The world-renowned African-American historian Lerone Bennett, Jr., has stated eloquently:

> Before 500,000 could march on Washington, D.C., before 30,000 could march from Selma, before there could be rebellion in Black America and renewal of the White Church, before SNCC [the Student Nonviolent Coordinating Committee] could sit in, before Stokely Carmichael could talk Black Power, before Martin Luther King, Jr., could dream, History (sic) had to take the flesh and form of certain Black men who were bold enough, wise enough and selfless enough to assume the awesome responsibility of preparing the ground for a harvest, the fruits of which they would probably never taste themselves.
>
> Of the handful of men called by History (sic) to this delicate and dangerous task, none tilled more ground or harvested a more bountiful crop than Benjamin Elijah Mays, a lean, beautifully black preacher-prophet who served as Schoolmaster of the Movement during a ministry of manhood that spanned some 60 years, 27 of which were spent as president of Atlanta's prestigious Morehouse College.

This graceful genius, one of the most creative architects of American education, is scarcely known to most Americans. He is rarely mentioned as one of the great American educators. Nevertheless, Benjamin Elijah Mays was a giant, and his influence touched men like John F. Kennedy; Lyndon B. Johnson; and Martin Luther King, Jr., who was one of his students at Morehouse College.

The name Benjamin means "son of my people." Mays was always involved in the lives of his people: not only in the halls of higher education but also in the everyday affairs of ordinary people, including those often forgotten. Often referred to as a "man's man," he was a genuine transformer, intent on bringing out the best that young men had to offer. One of Benjamin Mays's favorite statements was that he did not intend to make lawyers or doctors or teachers; he intended to make men.

Benjamin Elijah Mays arrived on the back pages of American history from very humble beginnings. He was born about thirty-one years after the Civil War, on August 1, 1894, in a small out-of-the-way place near Ninety-six, a county in South Carolina. His mother and father, Louvenia and Hezakiah Mays, were ex-slaves, poor sharecroppers who dedicated their lives to their children's well-being. Young Benjamin spent his childhood with a loving, close-knit family that included seven brothers and sisters. He never forgot who he was and where he came from.

Sometimes the importance of a personal goal is not endorsed by other family members. Even in an affectionate family like Benjamin Mays's, cultural values and financial circumstances will often dictate what a child should dream of doing with his life.

Formal education beyond learning to read and write was not important to some of the Mayses—because working in the fields to feed the family had to take priority. It was a matter of survival. For Benjamin Mays, the question was (as it still is for many who have a desire to learn and to seek a broader scope for their lives), what do you do when your family does not support your dream? Where do you go when the most important people in your life don't view the path you are taking as the right one? Do you forget about your dream and obediently accept the wishes of the family or do you rebel? Do you step out on faith without financial or emotional support?

Like many other talented people, Benjamin Mays not only confronted these questions, he found answers to them. Turn the pages of Benjamin Mays's life and witness his struggle to break out of the shackles of poverty and ignorance.

As a child my life was one of frustration and doubt. Nor did the situation improve as I grew older. Long before I could visualize them, I knew within my body, my mind, and my spirit that I faced galling restrictions, seemingly insurmountable

barriers, dangers and pitfalls. I had to find answers to two immediate and practical problems: 1) How could I overcome my father's immutable opposition to my insatiable desire to get an education; and 2) Even if I succeeded in changing Father's attitude, how could I get the money to go away to school? I knew that my father had no money to give me, but I longed for his sympathetic approval, or at least his consent. . . . My teacher in the one-room school, my pastor, and the church people at Mount Zion had inspired me to want an education far beyond what the four-month Brickhouse School could offer, and away beyond what my parents could possibly provide. How then could I get to a better school? How could I manage to remain in school more than four months out of the year?

My greatest opposition to going away to school was my father. When I knew that I had learned everything I could in the one-room Brickhouse School and realized how little that was, my father felt that this was sufficient—that it was all I needed. Weren't there only two honest occupations for Negro men—preaching and farming? My father must have repeated this dictum a thousand times. What did schooling have to do with farming? Would reading all the books in the world teach a man how to plow, to plant cotton and corn, gather the grain, and harvest the crop? Since my father saw no future for his sons except farming, education was not necessary. It was equally superfluous for the ministry. God "called" men to preach; and when He called them, He would tell them what to say!

Father had another reason. He was convinced that education went to one's head and made him a fool and dishonest. One of my cousins, a bright sixth- or seventh-grade scholar who taught at one of the county schools for the miserable salary paid Negro teachers during that period, forged a note on a bank, skipped town, and was never caught. He never returned to his home community. Later he joined the Ninth Cavalry. He wrote me occasionally, telling how much better the racial situation was in his part of Kansas than it was in the South. Whenever I pressed my father about further schooling, he would always remind me of what my cousin had done. The more education, the bigger the fool and crook! Though less literate than my father, my mother was far more understanding of my problems, and was a sympathetic listener to my hopes and dreams, my fears and plans. She had only two things to give me—her love and her prayers. She gave both with an open heart.

My mother believed that God answered prayers. Though not so credulous or optimistic about prayer as she, I was nonetheless greatly influenced by her prayer life. I sought a way out through prayer. I prayed frequently as I worked in the field and many nights alone in the moonlight. I often plowed to the end of the row, hitched the mule to a tree, and went down into the woods to pray. My prayers were all variations of the same theme: a petition to God to enable me to get away to school. My desire for an education was not only a dream but a goal that drove and prodded me, day and night. I left the farm not to escape it but to find my world, to become myself.

I accepted the prayer jargon of the older people. I asked God to move out of my way "every hindrance and cause" which kept me from getting an education. Afterward I was sorry that I had prayed that way, for if God had answered my prayers as spoken, Father would have been the first obstacle to be moved out. Since presumably God is not particularly interested in semantics, He probably knew that had I been wiser I would have asked for the will, the wisdom, the tenacity to overcome the obstacles that lay in my way.

So often the obstacles that confront us are not out there in the proverbial "society," nor are they racist or sexist demigods waiting to pounce. They are loved ones sitting at the same dinner table or growing up in the same household with us. Working and helping the family came first for this young man of so much potential who never attended school for more than four months a year until he was nineteen. It was not uncommon, at that time, for young black children to work twelve-hour days in the scorching, sun-drenched fields. Every able-bodied family member was expected to work and contribute to the family's economy.

It was truly difficult for this young man who loved and respected his father to go against his father's wishes, but education was young Benjamin's dream. He summed up his reaction to that episode with his father in these words:

"It must be borne in mind that the tragedy in life does not lie in not reaching your goal. The tragedy lies in having no goal to reach. It isn't a calamity to die with dreams unfulfilled, but it is a calamity not to dream. It is not a disaster to be unable to capture your ideal, but it is a disaster to have no ideal to capture. It is not a disgrace not to reach the stars, but it is a disgrace to have no stars to reach. Not failure but low aim is sin."

My father died in 1938. I am glad that he lived long enough for me to be graduated from the high school of the South Carolina State College, to earn a degree from Bates, to receive M.A. and Ph.D. degrees from the University of Chicago, and to become dean of the School of Religion at Howard University. While living with me in Washington, Father admitted his error in fighting my desire for an education, saying that he had opposed me only because he didn't know any better. But I had long since forgiven him; and it was my joy that from 1921 until his and Mother's deaths in 1938, in an atmosphere of mutual understanding and appreciation, it was possible for me to insure their comfort and well-being.

Other family and community members had believed that despite the obstacles of poverty and his father's restrictiveness, Benjamin was destined to do great things. From his first teacher at the colored children's school to the deacons and elders of Mount Zion Church, people had been viewing him as gifted, as having a future.

Benjamin Mays went on to do great things in the field of education and public service—this man who was nineteen when he finished his first full year of schooling, twenty-two when he finished high school, forty-six when he became president of Morehouse College, fifty-two when he was first allowed to vote, seventy-six when he became the first black president of the Atlanta Board of Education. And somehow he also found time in those years to serve as an advisor to Presidents John F. Kennedy and Lyndon B. Johnson.

He followed his dream. And in so doing, he became a leader and modeled the principle that "those who lead best, serve best."

Source: Mays, Benjamin E., *Born to Rebel.* Copyright © 1987. Reprinted by permission of the University of Georgia Press.

SELECTED READINGS

Graham, Stedman. 1997. *You Can Make It Happen: A Nine-Step Plan for Success.* New York: Simon & Schuster.

Kimbro, Dennis, and Napoleon Hill. 1991. *Think and Grow Rich: A Black Choice.* New York: Ballantine Books.

Mays, Benjamin E. 1987. *Born to Rebel: An Autobiography by Benjamin E. Mays.* Athens, Ga.: University of Georgia Press.

Stewart, Jeffrey C. 1996. *1001 Things Everyone Should Know about African-American History.* New York: Doubleday and Company, Incorporated.

QUESTIONS

1 *Have you experienced resistance from family members regarding your educational goals? If so, how did you handle it? If not, suggest some strategies a student confronting such resistance may be able to use.*

2 *Visit the library and develop your own profile of Benjamin Mays. Then compare his life with that of someone you happen to view as a positive role model.*

3 *Have family priorities ever interfered with your educational goals? If so, describe these situations.*

4 *What quality does Benjamin Mays exhibit that would assist you in finishing school? Explain.*

5 *Tell what message this story communicates to you.*

Kweisi Mfume (1948–)

President and CEO of the National Association for the Advancement of Colored People; former chairman of the Congressional Black Caucus

Conquering Son of Kings

A rare type of description, yes, but Kweisi is a rare type of man. If the simple task of changing one's name were all that it would take to acquire "substance" and "style," many of us would readily change our names. But we all know that it takes more than changing one's name or one's clothes or even one's job to build character. Character and integrity must be built on a foundation, and each person must have the patience, persistence, and insight to create that foundation and then build upon it. Kweisi built a foundation the hard way.

"Young lion . . . strong . . . elegant and bold" are just a few of the phrases that aptly describe this former member of Congress who became the president and chief executive officer of the National Association for the Advancement of Colored People (NAACP). However, a long time ago, "high school dropout" and "petty thief" would have been just as applicable. If any man represents true transformation with substance and style, it is Kweisi Mfume (kwah-*ee*-see oom-foo-may). All too often, substance has been sacrificed on the altar of style by would-be upwardly mobile Americans. However, as one observer has vividly stated, Mfume (who chose at the age of twenty-three, the Swahili name meaning "conquering son of kings") has the elegance of Duke Ellington, the eloquence of Martin Luther King, Jr., the brilliance of W. E. B. DuBois, the fearlessness of Thurgood Marshall (see page 52), the staying power of Nelson Mandela (see page 47), and the wisdom of Sojourner Truth.

Born Frizell Gerard Gray, he grew up in Turners Station, Maryland, a small African-American community in an area plagued with soot and fumes from the local steel mill. Many blacks from the Deep South had migrated to Turners Station, an enclave relatively safe from the poisonous tentacles of discrimination. It was a place that despite economic poverty was in some ways rich: a place where everybody was somebody, and everybody knew everybody else's business.

Many talented and delightful "performers" danced their way across this lively stage of yesterday. The sounds of jazz and gospel and the singer Billie Holiday could be heard as children laughed and played a local game call "Hot butter beans, come and get your supper." The sweet smell of Maryland fried chicken gently flowed through the air above the stench of industrial waste, while black families struggled together to make ends meet in post–World War II America. However, this idyllic-seeming place, like so many other African-American communities, was also the place that introduced Kweisi and his three younger sisters to the ravages of poverty and the pain of family disintegration. This place and this experience would provide materials for the foundation for Kweisi's life.

When Kweisi was twelve, his abusive stepfather abandoned the family. His mother struggled to keep the family together but when Kweisi was sixteen his mother died of cancer, in his arms. The family was grief stricken and torn apart. Kweisi, the oldest child, went to live with his uncle within Baltimore City, while his three younger sisters went to live with their grandmother. This seemed to be the beginning of the end.

Angry, disillusioned, and hurt, Kweisi dropped out of high school and began working at odd jobs. Before long, he was running with a wild group of boys. Like so many other young males, he was driven by a demon called anger. Unable to acknowledge and confront it, he became selfish, reckless, and even malicious. The deep-seated anger became a strong taskmaster that guided and drove his every action. He began to rob, steal, gamble, and drink. The anger clouded his self-esteem and blinded his understanding of love. By the time he was twenty-two, he had fathered five sons out of wedlock, by three different women, and was on a fast track to destruction.

This may sound like a Hollywood rerun about young African-American males who are angry, aimless, without hope, addicted, and lost. Well, in a scenario such as this, love *must* replace the anger, and hope *must* become a shield. For whatever reason, the anger has to be challenged if a life is to be saved.

As you review what you have read thus far about Kweisi, ask yourself what kind of foundation you have established for your life. How much have external circumstances helped you to develop that foundation? Is it a foundation of anger, deception, and blame? Does it need to be restructured or rebuilt? Could Kweisi have looked at the poverty, abuse, and family disintegration with a different eye? What can any of us do when our environment seems to be dictating our destiny?

Tired of the poverty, tired of the anger, tired of all the pain, Kwiesi sought change in the best way he knew: he sought God. He confronted God, and he admitted his anger. There was something cleansing and liberating about finally admitting that he was angry with God: angry about the death of his mother, angry about the destruction of his family, angry about the circumstances of his life.

In a 1993 article in *U.S. News & World Report* Kweisi said, "I was hanging out with the guys shooting craps and drinking wine.... And I guess until I die I never will understand what happened that night.... I just sensed it was my [dead] mother snatching me back to reality.... I felt cold on that very hot July night.... It was like the God I was angry with was saying that everything would be OK.... I left the corner, walked to my house, walked upstairs to my bedroom and got on my knees and started praying and crying and just asking for forgiveness. And I knew I wasn't ever going back to that again."

This experience forced Kweisi to break the downward spiral of destruction and prepare himself for a life beyond bitterness. It was the moment when he made a commitment to real, long-term, transforming change. He began a deliberate transformation of his life, a journey that would take many twists and turns but that would ultimately reveal his hidden strengths. He went to night school to earn a high school diploma and then to Baltimore City Community College, where he was a student government leader. He transferred to Morgan State University in Baltimore. At Morgan State, he involved himself with the struggle to free South Africa and spoke out against the ravages of racism wherever and whenever it had reared its ugly head. His interest in politics, African liberation, and music became an integral part of his self-made transformation.

After graduating from Morgan State with honors in 1976, when he was over twenty-three, Kweisi Mfume attended graduate school at Johns Hopkins University in Baltimore, where he specialized in international studies. Already, the concrete result of a changed heart, mind, and attitude was apparent in Kweisi. He was mastering his life and was on the right road to success.

Failures of the past do not have to generate failures of the future; and successful change can occur at the most unlikely time in a person's life. Change does not have a schedule, a calendar, or a clock; it just takes place when hard work and commitment are its foundation.

The heavy responsibilities of fatherhood, politics, and music began to dominate Kweisi Mfume's thoughts. He made a commitment to be a father in a true sense to each of his sons. He would pursue politics and music with a passion. He would work as a disk jockey and develop a reputation as a smart, talented, outspoken advocate of people's rights. In 1979, surprising many, he ran a grassroots campaign and won a seat on the Baltimore city council. The support he received was overwhelming. His constituents knew him, knew where he came from, and knew his struggle was real. After two successful but controversial terms as an advocate for poor people, he ran for Congress.

During this bitter and hard-fought campaign, Kweisi Mfume's past mistakes would be used repeatedly to discredit him. However, now politically mature and personally dedicated to a responsible relationship with his sons, he endured the storms of criticism, and with his sons by his side, he won the seat in Congress. (Who would have thought that a onetime high school dropout, petty thief, and low-level gang member would one day win the privilege to serve in the legislative branch of the United States government?)

Some say that from the moment he took the oath of office, he was determined to be a great leader who would win the respect and admiration of all members of Congress. His leadership in Congress was always in step with the needs of the people, not only in his district or state but also in the nation. He remained an advocate of the people even when he served on some of the most powerful and prestigious committees in Congress; and his reputation for getting the job done won him the coveted position of chairman of the Congressional Black Caucus.

In 1996, after winning major battles against personal demons and political foes, the man from Turners Station retired from Congress and became the president and chief executive officer of the NAACP. Kweisi Mfume, a "conquering son of kings," was embarking upon a new phase of his life and establishing the foundation of a fresh legacy.

SELECTED READINGS

Hutchinson, Earl Ofari. 1992. *Black Fatherhood: The Guide to Male Parenting.* Inglewood, Calif.: Middle Passage Press.

Mfume, Kweisi, and Ron Stodghill II. 1996. *No Free Ride: From the Mean Streets to the Mainstream.* New York: Ballantine Books.

Northrop, Henry Davenport, Joseph R. Gay, and I. Garland Penn. 1993. *The College of Life or Practical Self-Educator: A Manual of Self-Improvement for African Americans.* Chicago: C. J. Ayer Company, Publishers, Inc.

Stinson, Denise L. 1995. *The Black Folks' Little Instruction Book.* New York: Doubleday.

Name _____   Date _____/_____/_____

QUESTIONS

1 Does Kweisi Mfume's life speak an empowering message to you? If so, how do you plan to use that message in your life? Explain.

2 Examine several magazine advertisements and write a paragraph for each, illustrating how different styles (lifestyles, clothing styles, and other styles) are being promoted. What does this suggest to you?

3 Describe the biggest obstacle you have overcome in your life. How did you overcome it? Describe one of the biggest mistakes you ever made. Were you able to offset or rectify it? If so, how? How have your attitude and behavior changed as a result of having made that mistake?

4 List some skills or strategies Kweisi Mfume used to conquer obstacles in his life and reach his goals.

5 Has a name change or another special situation in your life meant a new beginning for you? Write a time line showing events before and after that event. Then write an essay describing the experience.

Alan Page (1945–)

Football Hall of Famer; first African-American Minnesota Supreme Court justice

From Jock to Justice

Alan Page has written a long legacy of accomplishments that many men only dream about, think about, and talk about. This man is truly a champion and is recognized among the best in three professional careers. Yet, Alan Page always remembers, regardless of what he is doing, that his long list of accomplishments is just that: accomplishments. They are not who he is; they are simply some of the things he has done. Read his story and observe a man who dared to challenge the odds. He refused to be limited by the boundaries of age, race, or other men. He prepared himself and took the risk to be different and to be the best. He understood that he was always more than the sum total of what he did or did not do.

"Fourth and one!" is a call very familiar to anyone who has played in the National Football League. Alan Page, the menacing defensive tackle for the Minnesota Vikings' notorious "Purple people-eaters," waits patiently, like a cougar stalking unsuspecting prey. The aches, pain, anticipation, and preparation all seem concentrated on this moment, a single moment frozen in time. A single play, this play, the last play of the last game of the season. Everything seems to be moving in s-l-o-w motion.

The ball is snapped; the quarterback smoothly and confidently backpedals to pass, but then, without warning, he quickly hands the ball to the stampeding fullback, who barrels his way through the hole of Minnesota's defensive line—but suddenly there is a hard crack, heard throughout the entire stadium by 50,000 fans, as helmets, shoulder pads, and two steel-muscled bodies collide. The roar of Minnesota's fans, shouting in unison "Alan, Alan, Alan," thunders approval as the six-foot five-inch future Football Hall

of Fame-er stands over his opponent and turns, lifting his gigantic hands in the air, gesturing, "We're number one; we're number one!"

Sometimes the roar of the crowd applauding success in one activity can hinder the hero's chance for success in another. If you have been an outstanding tennis, football, or basketball player—or a super scholar in high school or college—you may find it difficult to start any new endeavor at the bottom. As you read Alan Page's story, you will discover that he does not define himself by his accomplishments. Look instead for the principles and attitudes that have helped define who he is and what he does. See if some of those principles are guiding forces in your life. If not, consider whether you might adopt any of those principles, whether they could be useful on your road to success.

Alan Page played in the NFL for fourteen years, but if you were to walk into his judge's chambers today—he is a justice of the Supreme Court of Minnesota—you would not find a single souvenir of his stellar career in the League. What you *will* find is shelves and shelves of law books, along with some artifacts from the days of segregated America.

Judge Alan Page has been one of the most successful examples of someone making the transfer from professional athletics to a second career. He attributes his ability to move on, move beyond football, to the fact that he never let football define him. He has said, "I never had the identity of a football player. In my mind's eye, I was just Alan Page."

He was just Alan Page from a black middle-class family that strongly emphasized education. He was just Alan Page who set a goal to attend the University of Notre Dame—and did. He was just Alan Page who not only attended Notre Dame but graduated in four years, unusual for many athletes.

He viewed football as a job and as a means to an end. He was not, in his own mind, a jock or a superstar; he was just Alan Page doing his job. Eventually, he found football repetitious and boring. He believed that football was a finite game; that there were only a limited number of things one could do on the field; and that after about ten years, the average player would have done most of them.

While he was still playing football, Alan knew he needed a greater challenge for his intellectual and "warrior" instincts, so he enrolled in the William Mitchell College of Law in Minneapolis. Not realizing how tough it would be to combine the academic rigors of law school with the physical and emotional demands of football, he did not make a quick adjustment. After three confusing weeks, he dropped out of law school. He was one of the best professional football players in the game—but he was also a law school dropout. That did not sit well with someone whose family values had put strong emphasis on education. Still, as a professional athlete, he understood that a setback or a loss did not mean he could not play the game or win a championship. Sometimes the timing just is not right. You do all the planning and preparation—and still the pieces of destiny's puzzle do not quite fit together. But you do not quit. . . .

Alan did not quit. He made up his mind to return and face the greatest challenge of his life. After eight years with this unfinished dream haunting him, he went back to law school, at the University of Minnesota. This time, the planning and scheduling were right. This time, he did not underestimate the rigors and demands of law school and pro football. He understood that preparation and coordination would be the keys to his success, and this time, in 1978, he got his law degree.

He began practicing law part time while continuing to play, until 1981, when he retired from the National Football League as one of the game's premier tackles. He then practiced his second professional career full time.

Eventually, Alan Page joined the Minnesota Attorney General's office as a litigator. This was the first step in his progress toward becoming the first African American to sit on the Minnesota Supreme Court. Like a legendary hero, his response to competition, whether in football or in law, has set him apart from the ordinary, from the mundane. But neither his performance nor his prestige nor even his power defines Justice Alan Page. What does define him is his understanding of humanity; his everyday-ness; the strong work ethic his parents instilled in him; and his sense of fair play, which guides his pragmatic legal mind to battle a system that is not always colorblind.

Alan Page is a realist. He analyzes facts thoroughly and completely, but also moves with boldness and daring. He is an expert on moving from the place of comfort to the place of challenge. You see, Alan Page is not afraid to change. He was not afraid to step down so that he could step up. He has learned that no endeavor he is involved with has to be the final chapter in his life. Justice Page has indeed mastered the great skill of transition, the skill of moving forward with hope, because he is a pathfinder and a dreamer. Meeting challenges does make dreams come true.

He has had three premier professional careers; as a football player, as a lawyer, and now as a judge. Yet perhaps the most personally satisfying accomplishment has been creating the Page Scholars, an organization that awards grants to minority students who work with disadvantaged students in their communities. This is the power of one: that anyone can make a difference.

SELECTED READINGS

Cohen, Marjorie A. 1996. *World, Study, Travel Abroad: The Whole World Hand Book.* New York: St. Martins Press.

Marshall, Joseph E., and Lonnie Wheeler. 1996. *Street Soldier: One Man's Struggle to Save a Generation—One Life at a Time.* Delacorte Press.

Walker, Chet, and Chris Messenger. 1995. *Long Time Coming: A Black Athlete's Coming-of-Age in America.* Grove Press.

Willis, André C. 1996. *Faith of Our Fathers: African-American Men Reflect on Fatherhood.* New York: NAL/Dutton Press.

QUESTIONS

1 *Why does Parks reject gangsters as models of success? Is his definition of success correct? Consider professional athletes: they are often considered role models, but are they doing something worthwhile for society? Should they be held in such esteem?*

2 *Why is it important to be honest with yourself regarding the fulfillment of your dreams? How did the practice of positive motivation impact Gordon's life?*

3 *What is the difference, according to Gordon Parks, between intelligence and wisdom?*

4 *How did Gordon confront his faults on a daily basis? What are some strategies for confronting some of your faults? Why is it often easier to point out someone else's faults than to notice your own?*

5 *What do you believe was Gordon's greatest fear? What are some strategies you use to confront your fears? List as many as possible, then discuss three with another class member. See if your and his/her strategies are similar or different.*

Colin Powell (1937–)

First African-American chairman, Joint Chiefs of Staff

From the Ordinary to the Extraordinary

It was a clear fall day in 1991. Orange, yellow, and brown leaves colorfully decorated the vast promenade as the chairman of the Joint Chiefs of Staff rode along Pennsylvania Avenue in his chauffeur-driven vehicle. It was 0645, military time. It was not very early for the new chairman, four-star general, Colin Powell, who was accustomed to rising early. But this morning was different; it would be unlike any other in his entire military career. It was different, even, from the morning of his arrival in Vietnam during his first tour of duty, as a young lieutenant, even though that morning too was filled with excitement and mild trepidation.

Now, Colin Powell's mind was locked on to the objective that awaited him at the White House. His thoughts raced back and forth, covering every conceivable detail, analyzing every possible scenario, questioning every confirmed or unconfirmed fact that could make or break his case. And like a seasoned fighter or a great defense lawyer, he was prepared: ready for the sparring, for the skeptics, and for the barrage of toxic questions.

Nevertheless, he had a slight itch at the nape of his neck, and it seemed to intensify as he got closer to the White House. The starch in his shirt collar must be causing it. He certainly was not nervous, he told himself. He had met with the president hundreds of times before.

But this was his first private meeting with the president, and it would be the most important meeting of Colin Powell's hiterto unblemished and successful military career. Today President George Bush would say yes or no to an all-out assault on Iraqi President Saddam Hussein's forces. Thousands of hours had been spent preparing the top-secret brief on this issue that was for the president's eyes only. Men and women in remote corners of the world had risked their lives and jeopardized the safety of their families to obtain strategic information for this brief. And in doing so, they saved, possibly, thousands of lives on both sides of the Gulf War.

Colin Powell knew about sacrifice and struggle; he knew about tough decisions. It had been a long, arduous journey to his post as chairman of the Joint Chiefs of Staff from the multiethnic communities of Harlem and Kelly Street in the South Bronx—communities that had in many ways prepared him for this powerful position in the armed forces of the strongest military power in the world. This journey, his journey, had not been his alone. It was a spiritual journey, from the death of Crispus Attucks at the Boston Massacre to the sacrifice of every African American who had served faithfully and gallantly to protect the principles of the Constitution. This journey is the journey of all black people. It involved, too, the journey of Powell's West Indian immigrant parents, who had worked twelve to fourteen hours daily, believing that if they were honest and worked hard and treated other human beings with dignity and compassion, then their rewards in life would be plentiful and great.

Colin Powell had faith in his parents' values and put those values into practice. He worked hard; worked his way to the top. He earned each of his four stars, indisputably.

General Colin Powell's odyssey began on April 5, 1937, when he and his family were living on Morningside Avenue in Harlem. In the Powell household, education was almost as important as having faith in God. Education became the means that carried future generations of cousins and extended family members to a life better than what their immigrant parents experienced. As you read General Powell's account, you will witness how his family's values positively influenced his view of himself and how they spurred him to employ education as the vehicle for his own success.

The dominant figure of my youth was a small man, five feet, two inches tall. In my mind's eye, I am leaning out of the window of our apartment, and I spot him coming down the street from the Intervale Avenue subway station. He wears a coat and tie, and a small fedora is perched on his head. He has a newspaper tucked under his arm. His overcoat is

unbuttoned, and it flaps at his sides as he approaches with a brisk, toes-out stride. He is whistling and stops to greet the druggist, the baker, our building super, almost everybody he passes. To some kids on the block he is a faintly comical figure. Not to me. This jaunty, confident little man is Luther Powell, my father.

He emigrated from Jamaica in his early twenties, seventeen years before I was born. He left his family and some sort of menial job in a store to emigrate. He never discussed his life in Jamaica, and I regret that I never asked him about those years. I do know that he was the second of nine children born to poor folk in Top Hill. No doubt he came to this country for the reason that propelled millions before him, to become something more than he had been and to give his children a better start than he had known.

Education meant the difference between wrapping packages or sewing buttons all day and having a real profession. Education had led to an extraordinary record of accomplishment in my family. Among my blood relatives and extended family of lesser kinship, my cousin, Arthur Lewis, served as U.S. ambassador to Sierra Leone, after a career as a navy enlisted man. His brother, Roger, became a successful architect. Cousin Victor Roque became a prominent lawyer. James Watson became a judge on the U.S. Customs Court of International Trade. His sister, Barbara, was U.S. ambassador to Malaysia and the first woman assistant secretary of state: another sister, Grace, served as an official in the Department of Education. Another cousin, Dorothy Cropper, became a New York State Court of Claims judge. My cousin Claret Forbes, one of the last to migrate from Jamaica, is a nurse, with two children in Ivy League colleges. My sister's daughter, Leslie, is an artist with an M. A. from Yale. Yet another cousin, Bruce Llewellyn, Aunt Nessa's son, is a businessman, philanthropist, former senior political appointee in the Carter administration, and one of this country's wealthiest African Americans.

. . .

. . . My parents' first child, my sister, Marilyn, had been born five and a half years before [me]. I have no recollection of the Harlem years. They say our earliest memories usually involve a trauma, and mine does. I was four, and we had moved to the South Bronx. Gram Alice McKoy, my maternal grandmother, was taking care of me, since both my parents worked. I was playing on the floor and stuck a hairpin into an electrical outlet. I remember the blinding flash and the shock almost lifting me off the floor. And I still remember Gram scolding and hugging me at the same time. When my mother

and father came home from work, much intense discussion occurred, followed by more scolding and fussing. My keenest memory of that day is not of the shock and pain, but of feeling important, being the center of attention, seeing how much they loved and cared about me.

When I was nine, catastrophe struck the Powell family. As a student at P.S. 39, I passed from the third to the fourth grade, but onto the bottom form, called "Four Up," a euphemism meaning the kid is a little slow. This was the sort of secret to be whispered with shaking heads in our family circle. Education was the escape hatch, the way up and out for West Indians. My sister was already an excellent student, destined for college. And here I was, having difficulty in the fourth grade. I lacked drive, not ability. I was a happy-go-lucky kid, amenable, amiable, and aimless.

In later years, I would turn out to be a good student, but no one would have predicted it then. Marilyn continued to set the Powell standard in education. She had been an honor student at Walton High, and she excelled at Buffalo State. And so, in spite of my final high school average of 78.3, I started looking at colleges because of my sister's example and because my parents expected it of me.

Following Marilyn's example and Mom's and Pop's wishes, I applied to two colleges, the City College of New York and New York University. I must have been better than I thought, since I was accepted at both. Choosing between the two was a matter of simple arithmetic; tuition at NYU, a private school, was $750 a year; at CCNY, a public school, it was $10. I chose CCNY. My mother turned out to be my guidance counselor. She had consulted with the family. My two Jamaican cousins, Vernon and Roy, were studying engineering. " That's where the money is," Mom advised. . . .

My first semester as an engineering major went surprisingly well, mainly because I had not yet taken any engineering courses. I decided to prepare myself that summer with a course in mechanical drawing. One hot afternoon, the instructor asked us to draw "a cone intersecting a plane in space." The other students went at it; I just sat there. After a while, the instructor came to my desk and looked over my shoulder at a blank page. For the life of me, I could not visualize a cone intersecting a plane in space. If this was engineering, the game was over.

My parents were disappointed when I told them I was changing my major. There goes Colin again, nice boy, but no direction. . . .

. . .

Powell did not let his academic weaknesses short-circuit his dream. Since one road was closed, he simply looked for an alternate route. He discovered a different way to use his abilities. He did not let one miserable summer become a cross too heavy to bear. Acknowledging his failure, coming to terms with his limitations, he went forward.

During my first semester at CCNY, something had caught my eye—young guys on campus in a uniform. CCNY was a hotbed of liberalism, radicalism, even some leftover communism from the thirties; it was not a place where you would expect much of a military presence. When I returned to school in the fall of 1954, I inquired about the Reserve Officers Training Corps, and I enrolled in ROTC. . . .

There came a day when I stood in line in the drill hall to be issued olive-drab pants and jacket, brown shirt, brown tie, brown shoes, a belt with a brass buckle, and an overseas cap. As soon as I got home, I put the uniform on and looked in the mirror. I liked what I saw. At this point, not a single Kelly Street friend of mine was going to college. I was seventeen. I felt cut off and lonely. The uniform gave me a sense of belonging, and something I had never experienced all the while I was growing up; I felt distinctive. . . .

That fall, I experienced the novel pleasure of being courted by the three military societies on campus, the Webb Patrol, Scabbard and Blade, and the Pershing Rifles, ROTC counterparts of fraternities. . . . I pledged the PRs because they were the elite of the three groups. . . .

One Pershing Rifles member impressed me from the start. Ronald Brooks was a young black man, tall, trim, handsome, the son of a Harlem Baptist preacher and possessed of a maturity beyond most college students. Ronnie was only two years older than I, but something in him commanded deference. And unlike me, Ronnie, a chemistry major, was a brilliant student. He was a cadet leader in the ROTC and an officer in the Pershing Rifles. He could drill men so that they moved like parts of a watch. Ronnie was sharp, quick, disciplined, organized, qualities then invisible in Colin

Powell. I had found a model and a mentor. I set out to remake myself in the Ronnie Brooks mold.

My experience in high school, on basketball and track teams, and briefly in Boy Scouting had never produced a sense of belonging or many permanent friendships. The Pershing Rifles did. For the first time in my life I was a member of a brotherhood. . . .

The discipline, the structure, the camaraderie, the sense of belonging were what I craved. I became a leader almost immediately. I found a selflessness within our ranks that reminded me of the caring atmosphere within my family. Race, color, background, income meant nothing. The PRs would go the limit for each other and for the group. If this was what soldiering was all about, then maybe I wanted to be a soldier.

Colin Powell's Rules

1. It ain't as bad as you think. It will look better in the morning.
2. Get mad, then get over it.
3. Avoid having your ego so close to your position that when your position falls, your ego goes with it.
4. It can be done!
5. Be careful what you choose. You may get it.
6. Don't let adverse facts stand in the way of a good decision.
7. You can't make someone else's choices. You shouldn't let someone else make yours.
8. Check small things.
9. Share credit.
10. Remain calm. Be kind.
11. Have a vision. Be demanding.
12. Don't take counsel of your fears or naysayers.
13. Perpetual optimism is a force multiplier.

Source: From *My American Journey* by Colin Powell with Joe E. Persico. Copyright © 1995 by Colin L. Powell. Reprinted by permission of Random House, Inc.

SELECTED READINGS

Cox, Clinton. 1993. *The Forgotten Heroes: The Story of the Buffalo Soldiers.* New York: Scholastic Publishers, Incorporated.

Davis, Burke. 1991. *Black Heroes of the American Revolution.* San Diego: Harcourt Brace and Company.

Moskos, Charles C., and John Sibley Butler. 1996. *All That We Can Be: Black Leadership and Racial Integration the Army Way.* New York: Basic Books.

Powell, Colin, and Joseph E. Persico. 1995. *My American Journey.* New York: Random House, Incorporated.

Name _____ Date _____/_____/_____

QUESTIONS

1 How well do you think Colin Powell handled academic failure? What strategy did he use when he encountered difficulty in his mechanical drawing class? Explain your answers.

2 What was his attitude about college when he first applied? Does this attitude reveal clear purpose and planning for a career? Do you know of anyone who entered college with the same attitude? Has that person been successful academically? Why?

3 Why was Colin Powell's contact with the Pershing Rifles important to his college success?

4 Name some of Colin Powell's positive qualities that you could apply to your life. What positive or negative behavior helps or hinders your academic success? Create your personal list of "rules" that you live by and discuss your list with the class.

5 *How important do you think strong family values about education are, for student success? Why? How important is self-induced drive, in accomplishing one's goals in life?*

Susan L. Taylor (1946–)

Writer; editor-in-chief, *Essence* magazine

A Winning Attitude

Susan L. Taylor obviously has been blessed with a very successful life. She is the editor-in-chief of *Essence* magazine, the foremost publication for African-American women, and she is also vice president of Essence Communications, Inc. World traveler and fashion connoisseur, she shines like a rare and precious jewel, shaped and sculpted by her response to the trials and challenges in her life.

Susan Taylor's life has not been an easy stroll toward success. There have been many times when she has experienced disappointment, disillusionment, and near-despair. The plain truth is that through adversity, she has learned the importance of developing and maintaining a winning attitude—one that requires years of nurturing and cultivation. It is an attitude that must be consistently applied and trusted, even in the most difficult times. Susan Taylor's illuminating success is reflected in her faith in herself and her willingness to share her wisdom.

But the real question is, What made Susan Taylor respond to the trials of life with a winning attitude, when so many other people would have responded with grief and despair? Why did she become so different? As you read the excerpt from her book *In the Spirit,* consider these questions. Accompany her with an open mind and open heart; then embrace the wisdom she so freely gives.

I came of age feeling confident, capable and strong, as though I could do anything I chose to do. That was how I felt in my late teens, when I started studying acting and winning small parts. I had great self-assurance when as a young woman I completed cosmetology school and started my own cosmetics company. In my early twenties, with only a commercial high-school diploma and without any writing experience, my unwavering confidence led me to present myself at *Essence* for a job. The editor-in-chief at the time, Ida Lewis, believed in me because *I* believed in me, and she offered me the beauty editor's position.

But as my star began to rise at the magazine and I was promoted from beauty editor to fashion and beauty editor to editor-in-chief, my confidence began to waver. It seemed that once I reached the top spot I was invited to present myself everywhere from church pulpits to Capitol Hill and to speak about issues I wasn't well versed in. I could avoid those events easily enough by saying I was unavailable. But when my work began exposing me to more and more high-achievers, my self-confidence was shaken as I measured myself against the yardstick of these remarkable people's educational background and achievements.

I've been surrounded by some of the best minds and most accomplished people in the world: sisters and brothers who we would all agree have achieved greatness. They are heads of state and political activists; award-winning writers, editors and scholars; presidents of colleges and universities; great artists; highly talented actors, dancers and designers; the most beautiful models in the world. At times in their company I would lose sight of my own beauty and success. I would forget the enormous sacrifices that my parents made to raise their children and to get us through high school, and my own sacrifices and struggles as a young single mother on the career fast track. While I was greatly inspired by these high-achievers, there were times when I made them models of perfection, compared myself with them and diminished the wonder of my own life.

If maintaining self-confidence became an issue for me in my immediate world of supportive people who look like me, for sisters and brothers in environments where most of the images of power and greatness are White males—and where the structures and systems negate our achievements, intelligence and beauty—maintaining a positive sense of self can be an awesome battle.

When I started recognizing how comparing myself with others was undermining my self-esteem, I began taking periodic inventory of my achievements. While few of us Black folks were born to the manor, we often regard the struggle from where we began our lives to where we are today as "no big thing." For many of us, surviving our neighborhoods means not having gotten caught in the undertow of poverty, drugs and violence. If today we're in school or working, it says we're keeping our sanity in what are often hostile environments—while trying to move ahead, while taking care of family, friends and ourselves and the many tasks those responsibilities require. Given the many pressures in our lives,

the fact that we keep getting up and going every day is reason enough to celebrate.

What is your attitude about your life? Do you fully appreciate the distance you've traveled? Do you value your accomplishments? How we view ourselves means everything to us because it determines how we feel inside and how we move through the world.

While we must feel connected to the world around us so that we are able to function and interact in it, we must also remain independent of the superficial ways in which society measures success.

Our judgments of success are too often based on appearances. Through my work I've come to see that many wealthy high-achievers are also miserable people. We envy others' success without considering their struggles or pain. I measure success differently these days. Now I equate it with happiness, personal satisfaction and being of service to others.

If we feel "less than" in anyone's presence, it's because we are making assumptions about that person's life and not seeing our own clearly. And I can tell you from my own experience that when we continually doubt ourselves, we become divorced from ourselves, jealous and fearful.

We must remember that each of us is, as spiritual leader Olga Butterworth says, "a divine original." We are created by God to make a unique contribution to life, one that only we can make. This is as true for you and me, and for the millions who are unknown outside their small circles, as it is for world-renowned champions like Winnie Mandela, Jesse Jackson and Michael Jordan. The more actively we work at trusting and accepting ourselves, the less we'll compare ourselves with people we greatly admire and buy into the myth of our own inadequacy. If we want to feel confident, we have to make the effort to surrender self-negating habits.

We encourage a winning attitude by thinking and speaking about ourselves in loving and self-affirming ways. If you don't love who you are, but only what you wish to become, how will you ever achieve your goals? If you don't acknowledge your value or your winning qualities, how can you use them to achieve?

A negative attitude about where you are in life creates a losing cycle because you constantly criticize yourself, and that leads to self-doubt and feelings of diminished self-worth. We must admit our errors without deprecating ourselves or allowing anyone else to put us down. We should examine our lives critically and honestly, learn from our mistakes and try to keep a "getting up" spirit. Life wears us down if we don't keep ourselves up. I feel great when I'm striving for excellence and competing only with myself. I easily maintain a feeling of surety when I'm around affirming and positive people and when I exercise, rest, and do my spiritual work regularly.

When we're not meeting our own needs, we develop a negative attitude toward ourselves and life. This can lead to great unhappiness, all sorts of addictions and eventual mental illness. Through quiet reflection we develop the wisdom and courage to love ourselves as we are and to do the work necessary to create the self and the future we want. With a clear sense of ourselves, we make our own best choices, and by doing so we affirm our dignity and self-worth.

Source: Permission granted by the publisher, Amistad Press. Copyright © Susan A. Taylor, 1993.

SELECTED READINGS

Reid-Merrit, Patricia. 1996. *Sister Power: How Phenomenal Black Women Are Rising to the Top.* New York: John Wiley & Sons, Incorporated.

Taylor, Susan L. 1993. *In the Spirit: Inspirational Writings of Susan L. Taylor.* New York: HarperCollins Publishers, Incorporated.

Taylor, Susan L. 1995. *Lessons in Living.* New York: Doubleday & Company, Incorporated.

Vanzant, Iyanla. 1993. *Acts of Faith: Daily Meditations for People of Color.* New York: Fireside/Simon & Schuster.

QUESTIONS

1 *What does Susan Taylor mean by the phrase "models of perfection"? Explain. Why is it a disadvantage to have models of perfection? Are they different from mentors? Why?*

2 *Have you ever been in a class where most of the other students were high-achievers? How did you feel? What strategies did you use to maintain your own healthy sense of self-worth?*

3 *According to Susan Taylor, what is wrong with comparing and competing against others, rather than competing with yourself? Explain. Name some strategies you have used to build confidence and self-esteem.*

4 *Give your definition of a winning attitude. Give an example of a person who has a winning attitude. Explain why you believe he or she has one.*

5 *Draw a life history chart (time line) starting with your birth. Include all major events that have had a positive impact on your life. Also include your future goals, with approximate dates.*

Video Resources

Video Resources from the
University of Minnesota Film & Video Series
Minnesota Only 1-800-542-0013
Out-of-State 1-800-847-8251

Maya Angelou

Angelou, Maya, Creativity with Bill Moyers Series. DD 1L1378. 1/2" VHS.
Angelou, Maya, Rainbow in the Clouds. DD 100850. 1/2" VHS.
Wilson, August, In Black and White: Conversations with African American Writers Series. DD 100501.
    1/2" VHS.

Nelson Mandela

South Africa Today: A Question Power. DD 1S2345. 1/2" VHS.
Songololo: Voices of Change. DD 100132. 1/2" VHS.
I Shall Moulder Before I Shall Be Taken. DD 1S1796. 1/2" VHS.

Thurgood Marshall

A Nation of Law? (1968–1971) Program 6. DD 1H1292. 1/2" VHS ("Eyes on the Prize Part 2").
Power! (1967–1968) Program 3. DD H1290. 1/2" VHS ("Eyes on the Prize Part 2").
The Road to Brown. DD 1S2596. 1/2" VHS.
Thurgood Marshall: Portrait of an American Hero. DD 7H1382. 1/2" VHS.
Are You a Racist? DD 1S2398. 1/2" VHS.

Alan Page

The Black Olympians, 1904–1984. DD 7H1136. 1/2" VHS.
Black Paths of Leadership. DD 7H1134. 1/2" VHS.
Struggle and Success: The African American Experience in Japan. DD 100775. 1/2" VHS.
Color of Justice. DD 7S2717. 1/2" VHS.
Black Minnesotans. DD 1S2751. 1/2" VHS.

Other Videos

Kweisi Mfume

The African American Family, Images and Realities. Hosted by Danny Glover. Funded by AT&T, Distributor,
    Coby Communications, 1992.
African American Men, Images and Realities. Hosted by Louis Gossett, Jr. Funded by AT&T, Distributor, Coby
    Communications, 1992.
Black by Popular Demand. Thomas Furgerson, Redshoes Productions, Distributors: Music and Audiovisual
    Production Services, Des Moines, IA. 1988.